The Sagittarius Book
Everything You Should Know About Sagittariuses

CRAFTED BY SKRIUWER

Copyright © 2025 by Skriuwer.

All rights reserved. No part of this book may be used or reproduced in any form whatsoever without written permission except in the case of brief quotations in critical articles or reviews.

At **Skriuwer**, we're more than just a team—we're a global community of people who love books. In Frisian, "Skriuwer" means "writer," and that's at the heart of what we do: creating and sharing books with readers worldwide. Wherever you are in the world, **Skriuwer** is here to inspire learning.

Frisian is one of the oldest languages in Europe, closely related to English and Dutch, and is spoken by about **500,000 people** in the province of **Friesland** (Fryslân), located in the northern Netherlands. It's the second official language of the Netherlands, but like many minority languages, Frisian faces the challenge of survival in a modern, globalized world.

We're using the money we earn to promote the Frisian language.

For more information, contact : **kontakt@skriuwer.com** (www.skriuwer.com)

TABLE OF CONTENTS

CHAPTER 1: UNDERSTANDING SAGITTARIUS BASICS

- *Covers Sagittarius date range and Fire element details*
- *Highlights openness, honesty, and positivity*
- *Introduces the idea of restlessness and personal freedom*

CHAPTER 2: SYMBOL & BACKGROUND

- *Explains the Archer symbol (centaur with a bow and arrow)*
- *Describes Jupiter's influence and the Fire element's meaning*
- *Traces historical and mythological roots of Sagittarius*

CHAPTER 3: PERSONALITY TRAITS

- *Examines confidence, spontaneity, and humor*
- *Looks at deep beliefs, honesty, and tendency to speak directly*
- *Considers how restlessness and optimism shape their behavior*

CHAPTER 4: SAGITTARIUS IN FRIENDSHIP

- *Shows how they bond quickly and seek open communication*
- *Explores honesty vs. bluntness in friendly disputes*
- *Gives tips on balancing personal space with group fun*

CHAPTER 5: SAGITTARIUS & EMOTIONS

- *Reveals how they handle positive energy and occasional mood drops*
- *Discusses direct talk about feelings vs. private worries*
- *Suggests ways to share emotions without brushing issues aside*

CHAPTER 6: SAGITTARIUS IN LOVE

- *Highlights openness, need for independence, and honesty*
- *Examines dating styles, potential conflicts, and commitment concerns*
  Offers advice on balancing closeness with personal freedom

CHAPTER 7: WORK & CAREER

- *Shows how enthusiasm and directness shape their professional life*
- *Covers job-hopping, leadership possibilities, and need for varied tasks*
- *Explains overcoming routine boredom and building steady success*

CHAPTER 8: STRENGTHS & WEAKNESSES

- *Details honesty, optimism, and thirst for knowledge*
- *Addresses blunt speech, restlessness, and overcommitting*
- *Gives pointers to enhance strengths and soften tricky traits*

CHAPTER 9: COMMUNICATION STYLE

- *Analyzes direct speech, lively interaction, and humor*
- *Advises on phrasing opinions gently and active listening*
- *Offers tips on balancing frankness with empathy*

CHAPTER 10: LIKES & DISLIKES

- *Shows how adventure, openness, and variety appeal to them*
- *Explores aversion to strict routines, dishonesty, and dull tasks*
- *Gives insight into hobbies and preferred environments*

CHAPTER 11: SAGITTARIUS & OTHER ZODIAC SIGNS

- Explains compatibility with each zodiac sign
- Highlights shared strengths and possible friction points
- Suggests ways to collaborate or relate well with each sign

CHAPTER 12: SAGITTARIUS THROUGH THE AGES

- Looks at childhood curiosity, teenage independence, adult exploration
- Covers midlife adjustments, emotional growth, and older age pursuits
- Explains how the Archer spirit changes yet stays energetic

CHAPTER 13: SIBLINGS & FAMILY

- Discusses sibling rivalries, family roles, and boundaries
- Shows how honesty and freedom needs shape home life
- Offers ways to improve harmony while respecting independence

CHAPTER 14: FUN ACTIVITIES FOR SAGITTARIUS

- Lists creative, social, and outdoor pursuits to spark interest
- Includes ideas on group games, cultural exploration, and short trips
- Suggests varied routines to prevent boredom

CHAPTER 15: FAMOUS SAGITTARIUSES

- Profiles notable figures (musicians, actors, writers) under this sign
- Highlights traits like directness, reinvention, and global curiosity
- Examines how they overcame challenges or found success

CHAPTER 16: COMMON MISUNDERSTANDINGS

- *Clears up myths on bluntness, irresponsibility, and lack of depth*
- *Explains how honesty is not always harshness*
- *Suggests balanced perspectives to avoid stereotypes*

CHAPTER 17: HANDLING CONFLICT

- *Shows ways to resolve disputes using direct but calm speech*
- *Advises on pacing reactions, offering solutions, and seeking compromise*
- *Discusses group tensions, family fights, and work disagreement*

CHAPTER 18: SAGITTARIUS & SELF-IMPROVEMENT

- *Focuses on setting flexible goals, lifelong learning, and personal growth*
- *Covers beating boredom, combining discipline with freedom, and tracking progress*
- *Highlights managing emotional well-being and building healthy habits*

CHAPTER 19: SAGITTARIUS IN GROUPS

- *Explores how they contribute energy, fresh ideas, and motivation*
- *Addresses teamwork pitfalls like impatience or overcommitment*
- *Shows ways to balance personal freedom with group solidarity*

CHAPTER 20: SAGITTARIUS & FUTURE PLANS

- *Examines career paths, financial security, and big dreams*
- *Emphasizes blending optimism with practical steps*
- *Advises on retirement visions, adaptability, and making positive impacts*

CHAPTER 1: UNDERSTANDING SAGITTARIUS BASICS

Sagittarius is a star sign that people often link with big ideas, curiosity, and a cheerful way of looking at the world. It is one of the twelve signs of the zodiac. Many people feel excited when they learn about Sagittarius because it seems full of bright and hopeful energy. Individuals born under this sign have birthdays that fall between November 22 and December 21 on most calendars. While each person is unique, there are some general ideas that can help us get a better understanding of this star sign.

Basic Facts and Date Range

Sagittarius comes after Scorpio and before Capricorn in the zodiac cycle. When someone is born between November 22 and December 21, they are considered a Sagittarius, though exact start and end dates may differ by a day depending on the year. People often say that Sagittarius belongs to the group of "Fire" signs, which also includes Aries and Leo. This means Sagittarius is linked to strong energy, warmth, and a certain spark that lights up everyday situations. The element of Fire often brings a sense of enthusiasm and a lively mood. This makes many Sagittarius people seem like they are ready to share their bright ideas with others.

Enthusiasm and Interest in Learning

Sagittarius is widely seen as a sign that loves to learn about different subjects. They often enjoy reading, thinking, or having long talks about all kinds of topics, such as space, geography, animals, cultures, and more. Many people born under Sagittarius have a thirst for more information. This thirst can lead them to watch shows or read books to find out something new. They may also want to ask lots of questions to learn from those around them.

While being interested in many things can be fun, it can also make it hard for some Sagittarius individuals to decide which topic to focus on. They may start one project, then see something else that looks exciting and switch to that instead. This is not always a problem; it can show a bright spark that keeps them moving. Still, it can be helpful for them to learn the value of finishing what they start. By doing so, they can feel proud of all that they achieve.

Openness and Honesty

People often say that many Sagittarians speak their minds very openly. They might tell you what they think without hiding anything. This can be a good trait, because honesty is important when we want to trust someone. At the same time, it's a good idea for Sagittarius folks to remember that words can have a strong effect on others. While it can be good to share truthful opinions, it can help to be gentle with others' feelings.

This openness sometimes makes them wonderful friends for people who want honest feedback. If you ask a Sagittarius if they like your drawing, they might be very clear about what they think. Some might enjoy having a friend or family member who gives real and direct opinions. Others might find it a bit surprising at first. But with kindness and respect, Sagittarius honesty can bring trust and closeness in friendships and families.

Positive and Upbeat Mood

Sagittarius is well-known for being connected to hope and positivity. Many people who fall under this sign have a way of seeing life as full of possibilities. They tend to look for the bright side in problems. This can lift spirits for those around them, especially during tough times. For example, if a project does not go well, a Sagittarius might point out the lesson that can be learned or the small good parts that should not be overlooked.

This does not mean that a Sagittarius never feels sad or worried. Just like anyone else, people of this sign can have bad days. But they usually do not stay down for long. They often find a spark of hope or a reason to keep moving forward. This outlook can help friends and family members to smile and feel uplifted, even when things are not perfect.

Restless Energy

One common trait of Sagittarius is a restless feeling. This can mean they do not like being stuck in one place for too long. They often crave new experiences or fresh ideas to keep their minds busy. Some might change their hobbies often, switching from drawing one day to playing music the next. This can make them interesting companions because they are open to trying different things. It also means that, at times, they can grow bored if things do not change.

Learning how to handle this restless feeling can help Sagittarius people find balance. They might learn to turn their active minds toward healthy activities, such as sports, reading, or art. When they find tasks that keep them interested, they can focus their energy and still have fun.

Freedom and Independence

Another key point about this sign is a love of personal freedom. Sagittarius people often want space to explore their own thoughts, activities, or goals. They do not usually enjoy feeling tied down to strict rules or routines. Many of them like to be given room to figure things out on their own. This can be seen when a Sagittarius child might want to do projects without too many instructions, or a Sagittarius teen wants the freedom to pick what they wear or how they decorate their room.

This love for independence can bring a lot of creativity and self-reliance. At the same time, it's important to note that too much freedom without any guidance can cause problems, especially when it comes to responsibilities at home or school. Sagittarius people can grow and develop their own problem-solving skills when they learn to balance independence with basic duties.

Making Friends and Social Connections

Many Sagittarians are quite friendly and open to meeting new people. They might enjoy talking about all sorts of topics, from silly jokes to deeper thoughts about life. Because of this, they can form connections with people from many walks of life. They might go to school and quickly gather a group of friends. Or they might try an online activity group and meet people who share the same interests.

There is often a warmth to their social style. They like to laugh and have fun, and this can create a lively atmosphere around them. Still, not all Sagittarians are loud or outgoing. Some may be quieter but carry that same friendliness inside. The main theme is that many of them enjoy a sense of openness when it comes to interacting with the world.

Handling Feelings

While we will look more at emotions in a later chapter, it is good to note that many Sagittarius individuals like to keep a light or bright outlook. They might not always show deep sadness or worry on the outside. Sometimes, they prefer to shrug off heavy feelings. They might say, "It's okay, I'll handle it," even if they feel upset inside. This approach can bring a sense of calm, but it can also cause them to keep things locked away if something is really bothering them.

Because of this, it is helpful for Sagittarius folks to learn that sharing worries or talking about tough feelings is a good thing. Letting others know when they feel sad or stressed can help them find comfort and support. Friends and family might not always know how to help if the Sagittarius keeps everything hidden behind a happy face. By speaking up, they can find a healthy way to handle worries and other strong emotions.

Being Active and Adventurous

Many people link Sagittarius with an active lifestyle. This can mean different things, depending on the person. Some Sagittarius folks might enjoy sports, like soccer, basketball, or running. Others might like things such as dancing, hiking in safe places, or simply running around outside with friends. The key idea is that their lively energy can lead them to do things that get them moving or exploring their surroundings.

This love of action can also mean that they get bored if they have to stay still for too long. Sitting at a desk all day might make them daydream. That is not necessarily a bad thing, but it is worth noticing. It can be useful for Sagittarius children to find activities that let them use their energy in a positive way. For example, they might like group games, craft projects, or simple tasks that keep their hands or minds busy.

Creativity and Ideas

Many Sagittarians have a creative spark. They might come up with interesting art designs or stories. Their open minds can lead them to imagine many different possibilities. They might also be drawn to learning about philosophy or big life questions, though that depends on the person. The childlike sense of wonder in some Sagittarians can keep them excited about each day.

Because of this, they can bring fresh ideas to group projects or discussions in class. They might say, "Why don't we try something new?" This can be helpful when others feel stuck. The curious nature of Sagittarius can help them think of answers that other people may not think about. Even though not all ideas will work out, it is still fun to see how many possibilities can appear when they start brainstorming.

Challenges and Growth

Even though Sagittarius is often seen as a sunny sign, there can still be challenges. Sometimes, Sagittarius people might take on too many tasks at once because they find them all exciting. This can lead to feeling overwhelmed. Other times, they might promise more than they can deliver, because they believe they can handle everything. Learning to set realistic goals or to say no when needed can help them avoid feeling stretched too thin.

There can also be moments when a Sagittarius speaks so frankly that it upsets others. Being clear is helpful, but saying something in a nicer way can prevent hurt feelings. By learning a bit more tact (or kindness in words), Sagittarius individuals can keep their honesty while also showing care for the feelings of the people around them. With practice, they can balance that bright, open energy with gentle communication skills.

Why Understanding Basics Is Important

Reading about basic traits can help us see why some Sagittarians act in certain ways. Of course, each person is more than just their star sign. Other things, like family, friends, and life experiences, also shape their personality. Still, looking at these foundational traits can give us ideas about how to relate to Sagittarius individuals. If you have a Sagittarius friend or family member, you might notice how they light up when talking about something new they learned. You might also notice that they can't stand sitting around doing nothing for too long.

It can be fun to share interesting facts or let them lead a project. Giving them space to try fresh approaches can help them grow. At the same time, they might need a reminder that some rules are there for a reason. These basics help us see both the good qualities and some of the possible pitfalls of the sign.

Common Interests

Not every Sagittarius is the same, but some shared interests do pop up frequently among those born under this sign. They might like activities that let them be physically active, such as sports or playing in the backyard. They might also enjoy reading or watching shows about different countries, science topics, or animals. Their fascination with learning can lead them to gather fun facts that they can share with their friends.

They can also enjoy working on projects that allow them to get creative. For instance, writing a short story or making art can help them use their free spirit in a positive way. While they might shift from one interest to another rather quickly, each new hobby can be an exciting part of their growth.

Hopes for the Future

Because Sagittarius is associated with an upbeat mindset, many people with this sign have big hopes for what lies ahead. They might think about what they want to do as they get older and feel confident that they can reach their goals. This hopeful attitude can serve as a light that guides them through hard moments. However, it also helps when they set clear steps to make their hopes come true.

Doing well in school or practicing certain skills can help them later on. If they only daydream without taking small steps, they might feel stuck. That is why encouragement from friends, teachers, or parents can be valuable. A bit of guidance can go a long way, especially for someone who already has a bright outlook.

Finding Balance

Some people say that Sagittarius is like a flame that always wants to burn bright. But if it gets too big too quickly, it could get out of control. That is why it can be helpful for them to learn patience and steadiness. For example, if a Sagittarius child wants to learn a new instrument, they might get excited in the beginning but feel bored later. Sticking with the instrument through the basic lessons can help them see real progress. This teaches them that with a bit of consistency, their natural excitement can lead them to achieve a lot.

Finding balance can also apply to social situations. Sagittarians might love meeting new friends and talking to many people. But there are times when they need to listen just as much as they speak. By hearing others out, they can become more understanding and empathetic. This can make their interactions more meaningful, rather than just lighthearted chats.

Key Takeaways

When you look at the basics of Sagittarius, you see a sign that is full of zest, honesty, and curiosity. People of this sign often bring an upbeat vibe to the world around them, lifting the moods of friends and family. They prefer to speak plainly, which can be both a strength and a weakness. They love having freedom to do things in their own way, and they thrive when they are allowed to learn about topics that fascinate them.

At the same time, they can benefit from understanding boundaries and from being mindful of how their words affect others. They also need to remember the value of sticking with something, rather than rushing to the next big idea. By learning these lessons, Sagittarius individuals can make the most of their bright traits while growing in areas where they might struggle.

Moving Forward

Now that we have looked at these basics, we can see that Sagittarius holds a lot of charm. Each person will show these qualities in their own way. There is much more to learn about this sign, from its symbol and history to how it behaves in friendships, emotions, and work. Understanding these core ideas helps lay the groundwork for deeper topics. As we continue, we will see how the Archer symbol, the ruling element of Fire, and other factors come together to form a fuller picture of the Sagittarius sign.

This is just the first step in grasping the key features of this zodiac sign. For parents, friends, and even Sagittarius individuals themselves, keeping these basics in mind can make it easier to spot strengths and common trouble spots. It can also help us see why Sagittarians might act in certain ways that others find interesting or puzzling. With a solid base, we are ready to look at more specific details and stories that give Sagittarius its unique place among the stars.

CHAPTER 2: SYMBOL & BACKGROUND

Sagittarius is often represented by the Archer. The most common image is that of a centaur (half-man, half-horse) pulling back a bow to release an arrow. This picture has roots in stories that go back many years. The Archer symbol is not just a random shape; it has important meaning that helps us understand the spirit of Sagittarius. The sign also has connections to the planet Jupiter and belongs to the Fire element, each piece adding a layer to its character.

In this chapter, we will look at how this symbol came to be, the idea behind the half-human, half-horse creature, and why an archer with a bow and arrow fits the traits we see in Sagittarius people. We will also look at some of the background information about this star sign, including its place in ancient star patterns.

The Archer in the Night Sky

Like all zodiac signs, Sagittarius is linked to a group of stars seen in the sky. Long ago, ancient people looked at these stars and thought they formed a shape that looked like an archer or a centaur with a bow. While our modern eyes might have a hard time seeing that exact shape, early stargazers used their imagination to connect the dots. They picked certain stars and said, "This must be the Archer."

These star pictures helped people track the seasons and gave them a way to tell stories about heroes, creatures, and gods. Over time, this star grouping became known as Sagittarius. When we think of the Archer in the night sky, we are remembering an old tradition that tried to make sense of the world by giving shapes and names to the stars.

The Centaur Figure

A centaur is a creature from stories that is half-human and half-horse. Typically, it has the body and legs of a horse, but the upper part is that of a human. Ancient tales are full of centaurs, often describing them as wild or strong. In many stories, there is one centaur who stands out for his wisdom and kindness. Even though not all centaurs in myths are kind, the famous one in some legends is known for teaching and guiding heroes. This wise image is sometimes linked with the sign of Sagittarius.

Having a half-horse, half-human figure suggests the mix of earthly needs and higher thought. In simpler words, it shows that a Sagittarius can have an active, sometimes restless side (like the running horse), but also a thoughtful, curious side (like the person aiming the bow). This image reminds us that Sagittarius combines a passion for action with a love of learning.

The Bow and Arrow

When we talk about Sagittarius, the bow and arrow is a key part of its symbol. An arrow is something you shoot at a target. It represents aiming for a goal, reaching for something beyond your current position. This fits well with the idea that Sagittarius individuals often have big hopes or targets they want to reach. They look ahead, see something that inspires them, and try to move toward it.

The bow and arrow also show focus. When an archer draws back the bow, they must keep their eyes steady and their mind clear. This can teach us that while Sagittarius people might get excited about many things, they can learn how to focus and aim. With practice, they can direct their energy, just like an archer points an arrow at the target.

Of course, sometimes the arrow might fly off course, but even that can be part of learning. The important thing is that Sagittarians are driven by a sense of possibility.

Link to Planet Jupiter

In astrology, each zodiac sign is said to be "ruled" or influenced by a certain planet. For Sagittarius, that planet is Jupiter. Jupiter is the largest planet in our solar system. It is often connected with ideas of expansion, good fortune, and broad thinking. This lines up with the Sagittarius tendency toward hopefulness and a wide outlook. Jupiter's link to growth and abundance reflects the sign's love of new ideas and experiences.

Many astrologers say that Jupiter's influence encourages a cheerful and open way of living. It might lead Sagittarius people to make big plans and have faith that things will go well. On the other hand, it can sometimes lead them to go too far or promise more than they can handle. But overall, Jupiter's presence often brings an upbeat vibe that helps Sagittarians see a world full of opportunities.

Fire Element and Its Meaning

Sagittarius is one of the Fire signs, along with Aries and Leo. The element of Fire is linked to warmth, excitement, and direct action. Think of how a flame dances and flickers in a fire pit. It grabs your attention, lights up the space, and spreads heat. This is similar to how Sagittarius energy can fill a room with laughter and fresh thoughts.

However, just as fire can be tricky to control, the same can be said of Sagittarius energy. It needs healthy outlets. Otherwise, it might lead to restlessness or impatience. That is why many Sagittarians look for fun projects or group activities to release their energy in a positive way. The Fire element also suggests that they often have a spark of inspiration that can lead them to do kind things or share new ideas with those around them.

Early Historical Roots

The idea of zodiac signs goes back to ancient times in places such as Babylonia and Greece. People studied the movement of the sun, moon, and planets across the sky and noticed patterns. They created a circle divided into twelve parts, each with its own sign, symbol, and meaning. Sagittarius was one of these twelve sections. Ancient astronomers and storytellers came up with myths to explain why these star shapes were important.

Over time, different cultures gave their own spin on these signs. The Archer was a common thread, though the style might change in different regions. Even ancient Rome had myths and stories that touched upon the half-man, half-horse figure. Today, we still keep the name and symbol, even though our modern scientific views on stars have changed a lot.

The Meaning Behind the Half-Man, Half-Horse

Some say that the horse part stands for the physical side of life: energy, movement, and animal instincts. The human part suggests thought, reason, and the wish to understand higher concepts. Putting these two together might remind us that Sagittarius is neither purely logical nor purely emotional. It is a blend of passion and thought. This can be seen in how Sagittarius people often want to keep learning, yet at the same time want to stay active and try fresh activities. They may not want to be stuck in a place where they can't roam freely, but they also like to think deep thoughts and share them with friends.

Hope and Exploration in the Symbol

The sign of Sagittarius is strongly linked with looking around for interesting and different experiences. In the Archer symbol, the arrow pointing upward can represent the wish to rise above everyday life. Instead of staying still, Sagittarius energy looks up, focusing on what could be next. This explains why some Sagittarians might always be thinking about what's coming in the future.

Even the posture of the centaur drawing the bow shows an action that aims for something that is not yet here but could become real. This ties in with the hopeful and forward-looking nature of the sign. Many Sagittarians enjoy trying new things, whether that means reading about faraway lands or building a fun project in their backyard. This sign stands for the idea that there is always something bigger on the horizon.

The Link to Freedom

The Archer, free to roam, points to another important piece of Sagittarius: the need for freedom. A centaur is not stuck in one place. It can run in an open field, guided only by its own will. For Sagittarius, that open space is very important. If you imagine a person pulling back a bow, you can see that they need space around them to release the arrow safely and effectively. This is like a metaphor for the Sagittarius personality: they want room to move, to think, and to change plans if they feel like it.

This love of freedom can be exciting. It can also be a challenge for those who like strict rules. A Sagittarius might resist tight schedules or routines that feel too rigid. They might do better with a bit of flexibility in their day. Knowing this can help when working with or teaching a Sagittarius. Giving them a bit of space can help them do their best.

Myths and Stories

In some myths, a wise centaur taught heroes. He was known for his kindness, skill in healing, and knowledge of the stars. This may be one reason why Sagittarius is tied to learning and teaching. Though the sign does not only belong to teachers or learners, many Sagittarians might love sharing what they know, explaining topics that excite them, or guiding friends in a fun activity.

These stories have changed over centuries, taking different forms. But the main idea is that centaurs could connect the wild side of nature (the horse part) with the thoughtful side of humans. This balance can be seen in Sagittarius traits: a mix of wild energy, curiosity, and a desire to use their minds in clever ways.

Modern Interpretations

Today, you do not have to look at the stars to see the influence of the Archer symbol. You can find it in art, clothing, or even as decorations in homes. People might wear a necklace with an arrow if they feel drawn to the spirit of Sagittarius. Many also enjoy reading about how the sign's symbol can hint at personal traits, such as honesty, optimism, and a need for open spaces.

Not everyone believes in the zodiac or gives it much meaning, of course. But even for those who see it more as a cultural or historical topic, the story of Sagittarius is still fascinating. It is a reminder of how ancient people tried to explain their world. They used symbols like an archer or centaur to show the forces they felt in themselves and around them.

What the Symbol Teaches Us

The Archer can remind us of a few life lessons. First, aiming at a target can be a symbol of setting goals. Sagittarians might do well when they take time to pick a clear direction, draw back the bow of their will, and let the arrow fly. Second, the half-horse, half-human figure can show us that we have both a physical and a mental side. A balanced life respects both. And third, the energy of the Archer is meant to be dynamic. This reminds us that sitting still might not be the best use of Sagittarius's bright spirit.

Yet, the symbol also shows that aiming is just one step. You have to practice and refine your skills if you want to hit the target. This can inspire Sagittarians to be patient and consistent. It is good to be eager, but it is also good to remember that skillful aim often takes time and effort. In that sense, the Archer is both free and disciplined in a way that can help a Sagittarius person grow.

Misunderstandings of the Symbol

Sometimes people think that the Archer symbol means someone who is always moving forward without thinking about others. But that is not necessarily true. While many Sagittarians have a confident style, the Archer can also point to being a guide or champion for others. An arrow can be aimed not just at personal goals, but at helping the world around us. It all depends on the person's values and choices.

Another misunderstanding is that the centaur is always wild and untrained. While there can be a fiery side to Sagittarius, it can be channeled into positive acts. Wise centaurs in myths were known for teaching and healing. In the same way, a Sagittarius can use their energy to encourage others to stay upbeat and hopeful, not just to run around without direction.

Connection to Nature

The image of a half-horse might also remind us that Sagittarius can have a strong link to nature. Some Sagittarians feel most alive when they are outdoors, breathing fresh air or enjoying open spaces. They might love activities that let them see fields, mountains, or broad landscapes. Even if someone cannot go out much, simply having plants around or looking at pictures of natural settings might lift their mood.

This connection to nature can help calm the restless spirit of the sign. Being outside can give them a healthy way to use their energy. It can also spark new thoughts, since nature has a lot to show us if we look closely. The Archer's horse half is a symbol of a creature that once ran free in open fields. Many Sagittarians find something comforting in open surroundings where they can feel less restricted.

Cultural Appearances of the Archer

Beyond ancient Greece and Rome, archer figures appear in many cultures. For instance, in some Asian myths, an archer shoots down extra suns to save the world from too much heat. While that story might not directly link to Sagittarius, it does show how universal the idea of an archer can be. Many tales across the globe see the archer as a hero or problem solver who uses skill, courage, and sharp focus.

Though these myths might not always talk about the same traits, the general theme is that archers aim at something important. They believe they can reach it if they focus well. This is a powerful image for Sagittarius folks, suggesting they can find targets in life that match their hopes and shoot for them without fear.

Practical Meaning for Sagittarians

How does the Archer symbol and background help a Sagittarius in day-to-day life? It can remind them to look up and not get stuck in small worries. They can learn from the symbol to keep their sights on things that make them feel excited and motivated. It also shows them that focusing on a single target, even for a short time, can yield good results. After all, an archer cannot successfully shoot an arrow if they are looking in ten different directions at once.

When they feel frustrated, picturing the Archer pulling back the bow might help them remember that they have the strength to keep going. The energy of the Fire element, combined with Jupiter's influence, can be harnessed for good projects. They can bring light and warmth to the people around them, just like a flame gives off light in the darkness.

Putting It All Together

The Sagittarius Archer is more than just a nice picture for a star sign. It holds deep roots in myths and stories that go back many centuries. The half-man, half-horse body shows a blend of body and mind, while the bow and arrow point to aiming for something beyond the present. The planet Jupiter adds a sense of hope and broad thinking, and the Fire element brings life and energy. Together, these pieces create a symbol that captures the spirited qualities found in many Sagittarians.

By knowing the background of this symbol, friends and family of Sagittarius folks might understand them better. They can see why a Sagittarius might be bored if they do not have something to reach for, or why they might always look to a bright future. This sign is guided by a symbol that highlights boldness, openness, and a sense that life can hold many possibilities.

Reflections on Symbol and Background

For some, the zodiac symbols are just old-fashioned pictures. For others, they are a source of inspiration. Whether you believe in astrology or not, the story of Sagittarius can be a reminder that we all have something in us that wants to move forward and aim high.

Each time we set a target or think of a new goal, we are like the Archer.

Even children can grasp the idea of aiming for something they want to achieve, like learning a new skill or being kind to others. The symbol of Sagittarius can give them a fun image to keep in mind. Meanwhile, adults who like astrology might look at the Archer and think about how they can bring more hope and open-mindedness into their daily routines. In this way, the ancient archer in the sky still speaks to us now, reminding us to stay eager to learn and to aim carefully when we want to do something meaningful.

These details about the symbol and background of Sagittarius lay a foundation for many other aspects of this sign. Once we know the stories and ideas behind the Archer, we can connect them to how a Sagittarius acts in friendships, in love, at work, and in other parts of life. This chapter gave us an in-depth look at why the Archer is the perfect picture for people born under this star sign. As we keep moving forward through the book, we will see even more ways these traits show up in everyday life.

CHAPTER 3: PERSONALITY TRAITS

Sagittarius people are often known for a lively spark in their character. While there can be similarities in how they act, each Sagittarius has a special blend of traits that makes them unique. In this chapter, we will talk about different parts of their personality. We will look at how they manage day-to-day life, how they interact with people, and what drives them. We will also note some common challenges they might face. This chapter will not repeat what we have already covered. Instead, we will go deeper into the many sides of Sagittarius personalities.

Natural Confidence

Many Sagittarius individuals show a type of confidence that seems to come from within. They might step into a new situation—like a classroom or a community event—and stand tall without appearing shy. This does not mean they never feel nervous. Rather, they often trust their ability to figure things out. For example, if a Sagittarius child is trying a new sport, they might not worry too much about failing at first. They might think, "I will do my best and see what happens."

This self-assurance can be helpful because it gives them a boost when facing problems. However, there are times when Sagittarius confidence might lead them to jump into something without fully planning. While this can be exciting, it can also bring moments of disappointment. Still, their natural self-belief usually keeps them going, even if they stumble once or twice.

Spontaneity and Trying New Things

A fresh event or activity can attract a Sagittarius like a magnet. They often enjoy exploring fresh ideas, meeting new classmates, or taking part in different hobbies. They might suddenly decide to try painting one day or do some type of craft project the next. This is not always a bad thing. It can allow them to learn many new skills. Yet it can also become a challenge if they keep leaping from one thing to another before finishing what they started.

Still, this spontaneous way of acting can be fun for friends and family. The Sagittarius person might say, "Let's try a new recipe" or "Let's visit a different park in our neighborhood." This can turn regular days into interesting experiences. People around them might appreciate that sense of fun, as long as they do not mind sudden changes in plans.

Blending Humor with Daily Life

Sagittarius folks often have a lighthearted way of looking at situations. They tend to use humor to ease stressful moments. Even when things are tough, they may say something silly that makes others laugh. This does not mean they are unable to handle serious problems. Rather, humor is one of their first tools for managing daily ups and downs.

Using humor can help them and those around them feel better. However, a Sagittarius should be careful not to use it at the wrong time. Some situations call for serious attention. If they make jokes when a friend is very upset, it might come across as insensitive. Learning when to joke and when to listen closely can help a Sagittarius become a kinder, more thoughtful person.

Balancing Logic and Impulse

Sagittarius individuals often want to act fast when they see a chance. This can be very exciting, but it may also cause them to skip important details. For instance, if they receive an invitation to a school activity, they might say yes without checking if they already have other plans. This can lead to conflicts later on.

To handle this, many Sagittarians work on slowing down and thinking through their options. They might remind themselves to pause, read instructions, or ask questions before saying yes. By doing this, they can keep their natural excitement but also avoid mistakes that come from rushing. This balance does not happen overnight, but practice can help them manage their impulses better.

Morals and Strong Beliefs

A number of Sagittarius people hold strong opinions about right and wrong. They might feel a deep sense of fairness when they see someone being picked on. They might also have big ideas about helping others or making the world a better place in some way. This moral side of them can inspire them to stand up for a friend or speak out if they think something is unfair.

While this can be very admirable, it can also lead to tension if others do not share the same viewpoints. A Sagittarius might get frustrated and wonder, "Why don't they see what I see?" Learning to talk about differences of opinion calmly can help them keep healthy friendships, even when people disagree. Their strong beliefs can make them dedicated allies for causes that matter to them, which many view as one of their best traits.

Sensitivity to Criticism

Because Sagittarius people often feel sure about their ideas, they can be surprised or hurt when someone points out a flaw in their plan. They might take it personally, even if the person giving the feedback is just trying to help. This sensitivity may not always be obvious on the outside. Some Sagittarians hide it with laughter or act like it does not affect them.

Over time, many Sagittarians learn that listening to good feedback is part of improvement. Instead of feeling bad, they can focus on how it helps them. A friend saying, "Maybe you should do it this other way," can be a chance to refine a skill or handle a situation better. Learning not to take criticism as a personal attack can open the door to real progress for a Sagittarius.

Thoughtful About Big Questions

Many Sagittarians enjoy thinking about subjects that go beyond daily life. They may wonder about space, science, history, or human nature. This is often due to their curious minds. They might ask teachers or family members deep questions that others do not think about as much. This interest in big ideas can help them do well in school subjects that involve reading or discussion.

However, they should remember that not everyone is always in the mood to talk about heavy topics. Some people prefer casual chats. It is good for a Sagittarius to learn when it is the right time to discuss something serious and when it is better to keep things light. Finding the right balance helps them connect better with a variety of people.

Generosity and Giving Nature

Sagittarius individuals often have kind hearts when it comes to giving time or help. For example, if a friend is struggling with a homework project, a Sagittarius might offer to lend a hand. They like to share fun experiences and knowledge with others. This giving spirit can show up in simple ways, like offering a snack, or in bigger ways, like volunteering to help out in the community.

The key is to ensure they do not give more than they can handle. Sometimes, in their eagerness, a Sagittarius might promise too much help. They may want to assist everyone, but then discover they have no time for themselves. Learning to set healthy limits is an important part of growing up for a Sagittarius, so they can keep being kind without burning out.

Friendly Competition

Competition can feel exciting for a Sagittarius. They might enjoy racing a friend in sports or trying to be the first one to solve a tricky puzzle. Their natural optimism can make them believe they have a chance to win, which can be motivating. If they lose, some Sagittarians handle it well, laughing it off and saying, "Maybe next time!" Others might get frustrated, especially if they believe they had the skill to succeed.

Learning to handle both winning and losing in a fair manner is part of building good sportsmanship. Sagittarius folks who show grace in competition often become role models to others. They can say things like, "Great job!" to a friend who won, which shows maturity and kindness.

Need for Personal Space

One trait that can stand out is the Sagittarius need for personal space. While they might enjoy being around friends and family, they usually value having some time alone. During these moments, they can think, relax, and do activities they enjoy. This personal space helps them recharge.

It is important for those around a Sagittarius to respect this, especially if the person seems stressed. Giving them a little time alone often helps them come back feeling more balanced. However, Sagittarians also need to remember to rejoin group events, tasks, or family gatherings afterward. Striking a balance between being social and taking personal time is key to keeping their connections strong.

Adaptability in Different Environments

Sagittarius people tend to be adaptable, especially if they have not locked themselves into a strict plan. They might do well in different classrooms or clubs because they are open to change. For example, if they move to a new place or switch schools, many Sagittarians can adjust more quickly than others. They might see it as an exciting chance to learn something fresh.

However, adaptability can also lead them to switch plans too fast. For instance, they might have an art project in mind and then suddenly move on to something else the moment they see something interesting. While it is good to stay flexible, they might also need reminders to finish what they start. This balance between adaptability and follow-through can be a big focus for Sagittarians who want to improve their habits.

Calm Under Pressure

When a sudden problem comes up, some Sagittarius individuals can remain calm because they trust that things will work out. For example, if a class assignment is harder than expected, they might think, "I can handle this" and focus on finding a solution. Their hopefulness can help them keep stress at bay.

Other times, however, their calm might break if they feel trapped or see no clear exit. Because they do not like to be restricted, a difficult situation with no wiggle room can bring out anxiety. Learning coping methods, such as talking to a trusted person or making a plan, can help them stay calm even when the situation feels tight. Over time, this can become a powerful skill that keeps them grounded.

Ability to Cheer Others Up

Sagittarius people often have a natural gift for brightening the mood around them. They might tell jokes, share funny experiences, or simply show an upbeat spirit that makes others feel at ease. This can be especially helpful among friends who might be worried about a big test or a personal issue. The Sagittarius friend might say something uplifting or remind them of the positive side.

That said, cheering people up should not replace real listening. If someone is upset about a serious issue, the Sagittarius friend might need to pause and ask how they can help, rather than just telling them, "Cheer up!" By combining genuine kindness with their bright spirit, Sagittarians can be great at supporting others in a balanced way.

Attitude Toward Rules

Sagittarius folks can have an interesting relationship with rules. They do not always enjoy strict or unchanging guidelines. They might prefer to do things in their own way, especially if they think the rules are too tight. However, there are times when they see the sense in following guidelines, like when safety is important.

Over time, they may learn that certain rules exist to make sure everyone stays safe, fair, or organized. They might still prefer a relaxed setting, but they can do well once they see that not all rules are meant to hold them back. With the right mindset, they can become good at finding a middle ground between being free to act and respecting necessary boundaries.

Enjoyment of Challenges

A new challenge can get a Sagittarius's heart racing in a good way. They often love testing their abilities, whether it is learning a new skill or handling a puzzle. Their open mind and optimism can push them to keep going, even if the task is tricky. For instance, if they decide to learn a musical instrument, they might practice often at first, excited to see how quickly they can improve.

The challenge appears when they lose interest partway through. Staying motivated when the task gets tough is something many Sagittarians have to work on. Some do best when they set small goals and track their progress. This gives them a sense of achievement and keeps them engaged longer.

Approach to Planning

Sagittarius individuals might have a love-hate relationship with planning. On one hand, they appreciate having some structure so they do not forget important tasks. On the other hand, they do not want to feel tied to a strict schedule. They might say, "I will plan a bit, but let's stay flexible."

This approach can work well if they keep a simple checklist. For example, they could list three things they want to accomplish in a day, but not assign exact times for each. This gives them some structure while allowing room for that spontaneous side to roam free. Over time, they might find a middle path that helps them stay responsible without feeling trapped by their own plans.

Independent Thinking

A key part of Sagittarius personalities is the ability to think for themselves. They usually trust their own judgments, even if it goes against what everyone else is saying. This trait can make them stand out, but it also has a flip side. If they are too quick to dismiss advice, they might miss out on helpful tips.

By listening to others while still keeping their own viewpoint, Sagittarians can gain wisdom. They do not have to copy everyone else's choices. They can gather insights from different perspectives and then decide what works best for them. This keeps the independent nature intact but adds the benefit of learning from people who have good experience.

Dealing with Stress

Some Sagittarians handle stress by moving around or doing something active. They might feel better after a short walk or some form of play. If they are older, they might prefer a practical hobby, like cooking a simple dish or doing a craft. The key is to keep their energy flowing instead of letting stress build up.

Others might do well writing in a diary or talking with a trustworthy friend. Since they often have many thoughts racing in their heads, letting those thoughts out can be a relief. Discovering healthy ways to deal with stress is important for Sagittarius people, as it helps them stay bright and positive without ignoring real problems.

Deeper Emotional World

Although Sagittarius individuals may show a happy face, they also have deeper feelings. They can feel strong love, worry, or sadness, but might not always express these emotions in front of others. Sometimes, they prefer to handle their emotions in private or joke about them. This does not mean they lack feelings; they might just need a bit of time before sharing them.

In close friendships or family bonds, a Sagittarius can open up more. They may reveal their concerns, dreams, or regrets when they trust someone. Learning how to share these deeper emotions in a healthy way can help them form stronger connections. It also shows that behind their bright exterior, they have a lot of heartfelt thoughts.

Evolving With Time

As they grow older, many Sagittarians learn from their mistakes and become more balanced. They might start by acting on impulse all the time, then realize they need a little more planning. They might speak openly in every situation, then see the value of kindness in tough conversations. With each lesson, they can refine their traits without losing their natural spark.

This does not mean they completely change who they are. Instead, they find ways to make the most of their strengths while handling their weaknesses with care. For instance, a Sagittarius who used to be overly frank might learn to phrase things gently. They keep their honesty but add empathy. This growth can make them strong and caring individuals.

Harmony With Others

Sagittarians often get along well with people who appreciate honesty and a bit of adventure. They might form friendships with those who like to explore ideas or try new things. However, they can clash with those who prefer rigid order or do not enjoy discussing different viewpoints. Even then, a Sagittarius who has learned to respect differences can still maintain friendly ties with people who see the world differently.

Harmony does not mean they must become someone else. Instead, they can look for shared interests or set healthy boundaries. For example, if a friend is very cautious, the Sagittarius might offer small steps toward something new, rather than pushing them too hard. By doing this, they show respect for each person's comfort level, which helps maintain positive relationships.

Leadership Potential

Because of their confidence, cheerfulness, and interest in big ideas, many Sagittarians have natural leadership potential. They might volunteer to lead a group project or act as a mentor to younger kids in some setting. Their optimism can inspire others to keep going, even if the task is difficult.

However, leadership also requires listening, patience, and organization. If they rush forward without including everyone's thoughts, their team might feel overlooked. So, a Sagittarius leader does best when they actively involve others. They can channel their drive into planning, guiding, and uplifting the group, rather than just running ahead alone.

Enjoying Simple Moments

Even though Sagittarians often think about grand ideas, they can still enjoy simple moments. They might love a cozy evening reading a good book or playing a card game with friends. These small pleasures give them a break from their active minds. They can laugh at a silly joke or appreciate a peaceful walk outside.

Recognizing these small joys helps them avoid feeling bored when big events are not happening. It can also help them see that life is not only about big projects or achievements. By learning to relax and find delight in everyday things, they become more balanced and content.

Respect for Different Cultures and Beliefs

Many Sagittarians show respect and interest in different cultures, languages, or belief systems. They might watch videos about life in other parts of the world or read stories set in distant places. This curiosity can make them open-minded. They see variety as something that enriches life.

At the same time, it is good for them to remember that not everyone shares their curiosity. Some might prefer sticking to what they know. A mature Sagittarius can gently share new ideas without pushing them onto others. Respect is key, and it becomes a two-way street when they also listen to why others hold different beliefs.

Conclusion

Sagittarius personalities include a broad range of qualities: confidence, spontaneity, kindness, a thirst for ideas, and a strong sense of fairness. They might face challenges with staying focused or managing their blunt speaking style, but they have the potential to grow in these areas. By combining their bright outlook with a willingness to learn, they can become well-rounded individuals.

While not every Sagittarius will show every trait, these themes commonly appear. As they get older, they find ways to direct their strong energy and share their warmth with others. The end goal is not to remove their lively nature, but to shape it so it works well in daily life. This chapter offers a peek at the deeper layers of Sagittarius behavior, giving us a clearer idea of what makes them tick.

CHAPTER 4: SAGITTARIUS IN FRIENDSHIP

Friendship is an important part of life for many Sagittarians, who often thrive in social settings. They enjoy meeting people, talking about ideas, and having fun in group activities. In this chapter, we will talk about how Sagittarius people behave with their friends, how they handle problems in friendships, and what sorts of connections they tend to form. We will look at how their personality affects these relationships, without repeating earlier sections. This chapter will cover new ideas about friendships, group dynamics, and healthy social habits.

A Welcoming Approach

Sagittarius people are often welcoming when meeting someone for the first time. They might greet newcomers with a big smile or a friendly remark. Because of this, they can make new friends quickly. A Sagittarius child on the playground might wave at someone sitting alone and invite them to join a game. This openness helps others feel included right away.

At the same time, they do not enjoy friendships that are full of limits or tight rules. They prefer connections where they can be themselves. This can lead them to form bonds with people who are also relaxed and accepting. If a friendship becomes too rigid, a Sagittarius may feel the need to step back.

Sharing Ideas With Friends

Sagittarius individuals like to talk about various topics, from silly stories to more serious subjects. They might ask their friends: "What do you think about this?" or "Have you heard about that?" They enjoy hearing different opinions, and they like sharing their own. This can make conversations lively and interesting.

In group settings, a Sagittarius might be the one who says something thought-provoking to get everyone talking. Friends can find this exciting, but it can also be a lot to handle if not everyone wants to discuss heavy topics. A Sagittarius learns over time how to read the mood of a group. They can adjust and keep the conversation at a level that fits the moment.

Honesty Among Friends

When it comes to friendships, many Sagittarians place a high value on honesty. If a friend asks for an opinion, the Sagittarius might give a direct answer. This can be refreshing because friends know they are getting a real viewpoint rather than a made-up response. Yet it can also lead to hurt feelings if the feedback is not delivered carefully.

A wise Sagittarius friend might learn to say, "I think you can improve here, but I still believe in you," rather than being too blunt. Mastering this balance helps them maintain good friendships, as honest feedback will be more easily accepted if it is kind. By respecting their friends' feelings, they keep the door open for deeper trust and support.

Leading Fun Group Activities

Since Sagittarius folks often have lots of energy and ideas, they might be the friend who organizes fun activities. They could plan a small craft event or suggest trying a new sport. Because of their upbeat nature, others often join in eagerly. This can turn an ordinary afternoon into a good time for everyone.

However, a Sagittarius might also feel frustrated if nobody wants to participate in their idea. Sometimes, friends have other plans or might just want to rest. A patient Sagittarius learns that not every idea has to happen right away. They also learn to let friends take the lead at times. Sharing the spotlight can help the group feel balanced.

Encouraging Friendships Across Different Groups

Sagittarius individuals like variety, so they might have friends in different circles—sports teams, art clubs, or online groups. They often feel comfortable inviting these different groups to mix. For example, they might say, "Let's hang out together, and I'll introduce you to my friend from drama class." This can lead to bigger, more diverse friend circles.

While this can be fun, it can also bring unexpected challenges. Different groups of friends may not always get along or share similar interests. A Sagittarius who wants everyone to blend might feel sad if there is tension between groups. Over time, they learn that not everyone will become instant friends, but they still maintain each bond in its own way.

Dealing With Disagreements

Disagreements are normal in any friendship, and Sagittarians have their own way of handling them. They may be straightforward, saying exactly how they feel. This can solve problems quickly if both sides are open to talking things through. However, if the other person is upset by blunt words, it might take more time to fix the situation.

Sagittarius folks who take a moment to think before speaking often have better outcomes. They can say, "I need to share my thoughts on this, but I want to respect your feelings." This approach can keep a small argument from turning into a bigger issue. Keeping lines of communication open is key.

Trust and Dependability

Although Sagittarians like freedom, they do not want to let down their true friends. Once a Sagittarius truly cares about someone, they do their best to be there for that friend. If a friend needs to talk or share a concern, the Sagittarius may offer an open ear. However, they might struggle with smaller tasks, like remembering a meeting time or giving a reminder call, because details are not always their strong suit.

Their friends may notice that a Sagittarius's heart is in the right place, even if they occasionally forget minor plans. Over time, a Sagittarius can learn to set simple reminders. This helps them prove to their friends that they can be counted on, both for emotional support and for keeping promises.

Enjoying the Lighter Side of Life Together

A Sagittarius often loves to crack jokes or propose silly activities with friends. Playing group games, watching comedy shows, or having friendly contests can bring them closer. These easygoing moments help both parties relax. The Sagittarius sense of humor is a big plus in friendships, lifting the spirit of the group.

One caution is that sometimes serious issues might need to be addressed, and a Sagittarius might default to laughter. While laughter is helpful, it does not solve major problems. Knowing when to be lighthearted and when to be serious allows them to be a stronger friend who can handle both fun times and real issues.

Handling Secret-Keeping

In friendships, people often share secrets or personal stories. Sagittarius individuals might find it a bit challenging to hold onto secrets, not because they want to gossip, but because they like talking and sharing what they know. If they are not careful, they might accidentally reveal something that was meant to be private.

Learning to keep a friend's secret safe is an important lesson. A friend should be able to trust that sensitive information will not spread. A Sagittarius who respects this boundary can build stronger bonds. They might say, "Thank you for trusting me. I promise not to tell anyone else." This kind of reassurance can bring peace of mind to the friend who opened up.

Offering Encouragement

Sagittarius friends are often good at lifting others when they are feeling down. They might say supportive words or focus on solutions rather than problems. This can help a friend see the positive side. Their own hopeful outlook can be a source of comfort for those around them.

However, sometimes a friend just needs someone to listen quietly. If a Sagittarius keeps trying to "fix" the situation right away, it might feel like they are overlooking the friend's feelings. Balancing active support with calm understanding makes a Sagittarius even more valuable as a friend. Simply sitting with someone and letting them speak can be just as helpful as giving advice.

Respecting Personal Boundaries

Because Sagittarius enjoys action and excitement, they might push friends to do new things. This can be a good form of encouragement. But if a friend truly does not want to try something, repeatedly pushing can create tension. A friend might say, "I appreciate the idea, but I don't feel comfortable doing that."

A considerate Sagittarius will respect this and avoid nagging. They can learn to read nonverbal cues. If a friend looks uneasy, it might be time to switch plans. By honoring personal comfort zones, they keep friendships healthy.

Being Open to Apologies

No matter how close friends are, misunderstandings can occur. A Sagittarius might accidentally say something that offends someone or forget an important day. What matters is how they handle it afterward. Apologizing openly can fix many problems. Saying something like, "I realize I messed up, and I am really sorry," can go a long way.

Because they value honesty, many Sagittarians will admit their error if they realize they have hurt someone's feelings. This direct approach can restore friendship bonds faster than pretending nothing happened. Over time, they may become skilled at apologizing in a warm, sincere way.

Accepting Differences in Friends

A Sagittarius often gathers friends from different backgrounds or with different interests. They might find one friend who loves sports, another friend who loves art, and another who loves computers. They see something interesting in each person. This variety can lead to a wide range of shared experiences.

However, differences in personality or interests can also lead to small clashes, especially if friends cannot find middle ground. The Sagittarius might realize that they have to plan different activities for each friend group. This is not a bad thing; it just means they understand each friendship has its own unique flavor. By valuing what each friend brings, they keep those friendships strong.

Long-Distance Friendships

Sagittarians often stay in touch with people even if they are far away. Because they like to learn about all sorts of things, they might exchange messages, photos, or stories with friends who live elsewhere. They enjoy hearing what is going on in different places. If a friend moves away or if they move themselves, they might still remain close through calls or online chats.

The challenge is remembering to keep in touch regularly. A Sagittarius might get busy with local friends or fresh interests and accidentally neglect old friends. Setting a reminder or scheduling a quick call can help keep important connections from fading. This small effort can show a friend that they still matter, even at a distance.

Teaming Up With Friends for Good Causes

Sagittarius people often have a sense of fairness and can be drawn to helping others. They might gather friends to volunteer or help in the community. They could organize a simple donation drive or find fun ways to raise support for a school event. Because they bring enthusiasm, they can spark their friends' interest too.

However, they should also be ready to handle the details behind these efforts. For instance, if they plan a bake sale to help a local group, they might need to confirm the location, timing, and who is baking what. This is where having detail-oriented friends can help. By working together, they can combine the Sagittarius spark with practical planning to achieve good results.

Supporting Each Other's Goals

Friends often help each other set or reach goals. A Sagittarius might say to a friend, "I believe you can do it!" This can give that friend extra confidence. In turn, the friend can remind the Sagittarius to stick with their own goals, such as finishing a creative project or practicing a skill. This mutual support can be a lovely part of their bond.

Sagittarius individuals sometimes get distracted. They might love having a friend who keeps track of things like deadlines or steps in a process. That way, the Sagittarius can enjoy the big-picture thinking while their friend helps with the details. Both sides benefit from the teamwork.

Staying True to Oneself in Friendships

One of the best parts of a strong friendship is feeling free to be yourself. Sagittarians value honesty, so they generally dislike putting on an act to impress someone. They want their friends to accept them as they are—energetic, a bit outspoken, and full of ideas.

In return, they try to accept their friends' real selves. They might say, "You do not have to pretend around me." This acceptance can lead to a deep sense of trust. Friends know they do not have to hide what they like or fear. The friend and the Sagittarius can share common ground without judgment. This genuine acceptance is a big reason Sagittarians are often well-loved by their close pals.

Watching Out for Overconfidence in Friendships

Because Sagittarians can be confident and full of ideas, they might accidentally overshadow friends who are quieter. A shy friend could feel ignored if the Sagittarius is always the center of attention.

Sometimes, a Sagittarius might be so excited about telling a story that they forget to ask about how their friend's day went.

Learning to take a step back and say, "How about you? How are things going for you?" can help balance the friendship. By showing genuine interest in others, a Sagittarius becomes a better companion. Over time, they may realize that letting friends take the spotlight now and then creates stronger bonds.

Comfort in Casual Gatherings

Sagittarius folks often thrive in casual settings. They might enjoy a picnic or a simple get-together at someone's house, rather than a fancy event with rigid rules. In these relaxed spaces, they can chat freely, make jokes, and move around without feeling held back. Friends who share this preference might find the Sagittarius friend to be a perfect match for low-stress socializing.

However, it is still good for Sagittarians to practice basic manners for more formal occasions. If a friend's event calls for certain courtesies, the Sagittarius might need to be more restrained. Being able to adapt to both casual and formal settings is a useful social skill that keeps friendships strong, no matter where they end up spending time together.

Handling Friendship Breakdowns

Sadly, not every friendship lasts forever. Sometimes, paths split or misunderstandings grow. A Sagittarius might feel confused if a friend withdraws or if they cannot reach an agreement. Their reaction might be a mix of sadness, anger, or even some relief, depending on the situation.

Handling a friendship breakdown can be tough, but it is a chance to learn. A Sagittarius might look back and ask, "What went wrong?

Could I have done something differently?" This self-examination can help them avoid similar mistakes in the future. If the other person is open to it, they might talk things out. If not, the Sagittarius can still hold onto the positive memories and keep moving forward.

Being a Reliable Shoulder to Lean On

When a friend faces a big problem—like loss, fear, or heartbreak—Sagittarians can be very caring if they tune in. Their hopeful nature might help the friend see a small bright spot in a dark time. They might share encouraging words or simply offer to spend time together, so the friend does not feel alone.

Still, they should remember that not every problem can be quickly solved. Sometimes, a friend needs more than cheerful words. They might need calm support or someone who can just sit quietly and share the load. Balancing their bright spirit with gentle care can make a Sagittarius a great source of comfort.

Discovering Shared Adventures

Many Sagittarians love finding shared activities with their friends, whether it is playing games, discovering new music, or learning a craft. This can strengthen the bond between them. Together, they can find fun things to do on weekends or after school. They might form clubs for things they both enjoy.

Because they get bored easily, a Sagittarius might constantly look for fresh things to do with friends. As long as their friends are open to changing routines, it can lead to plenty of happy memories. However, some friends might prefer simpler, quieter activities. A thoughtful Sagittarius will remember to ask, "Is everyone okay with this plan?" instead of rushing ahead with their own ideas.

Being Protective

When a Sagittarius cares deeply about a friend, they can become quite protective. If someone threatens or bullies that friend, the Sagittarius may quickly step in. They might tell the bully to stop or encourage the friend to speak up. This protective side shows how seriously a Sagittarius values their friendships.

Of course, they should ensure they do not start unnecessary conflicts. Sometimes, calmly reporting an issue to a trusted adult is better than confronting someone head-on. Being protective is good, but it should be handled in a responsible way.

Helping Friends Grow

Sagittarius individuals often have a knack for helping friends see possibilities. If a friend is unsure about trying out for a play or joining a team, the Sagittarius might say, "You should go for it. You never know what might happen." This boost can push the friend to discover new abilities or gain confidence.

However, it is important for a Sagittarius to recognize if a friend genuinely does not want to do something. Pushing someone too hard can cause stress. The best kind of help is encouraging them to consider it, while still respecting their personal choice. That way, everyone feels free but also supported.

CHAPTER 5: SAGITTARIUS & EMOTIONS

Emotions are an important part of everyone's life, and Sagittarius individuals are no exception. They often show bright energy and optimism, yet they also have quieter or more delicate feelings underneath. While we have mentioned some emotional traits in earlier chapters, here we will look more closely at how Sagittarians manage their emotions, express feelings, and respond to emotional situations around them. We will introduce new details to avoid repeating what was covered in previous chapters.

Openness vs. Private Feelings

At first glance, many Sagittarians can appear fully open with their emotions. They might smile, laugh, and talk about their excitement without hesitation. They are not always shy about showing when they are happy or amused. However, when it comes to heavier emotions—such as deep sadness, fear, or shame—some Sagittarians can become more private.

They may hide these heavier emotions behind humor or distraction. For example, if something makes them upset, they might crack jokes to shift focus. This does not mean they do not feel deeply. It only means they sometimes prefer to handle those heavier emotions on their own or in a safe, quiet setting. Over time, they can learn that sharing worries or sadness with someone they trust can bring relief, rather than feeling like a weakness.

Emotional Highs and Lows

Sagittarius is a Fire sign, often linked with lively energy. In terms of emotions, that can look like high peaks of excitement or bursts of enthusiasm. They may become very happy about a new idea, an upcoming event, or even a small positive change in their everyday routine. This bright excitement can be contagious, causing those around them to share in their energy.

On the flip side, when disappointment hits, it might feel like a strong drop in mood. Because they put a lot of hope into their ideas and plans, failure or rejection can sting more than they let on. Still, they usually bounce back quickly, thanks to their strong sense of hope. They do not enjoy staying in a sad or dark mood for long if they can help it. This bounce-back ability can be both a gift and a challenge: while it is great they can recover, sometimes they may move on too quickly and not fully process lessons from the setback.

Humor as a Shield

Sagittarians have a well-known sense of humor. They often use laughter to make social situations lighter or to set people at ease. But sometimes they also use humor as a shield to avoid showing vulnerability. For example, if a Sagittarius feels worried before a big exam, they might act silly or crack jokes to hide how tense they are.

In small doses, this can be a good coping strategy. It keeps their mind from dwelling on the negative. However, if humor always replaces honest emotional sharing, it might prevent them from feeling understood by friends or family. Learning when it is time to set jokes aside and say, "I am actually a bit scared," can help them form stronger emotional bonds with others.

Quick Anger and Quick Forgiveness

Some Sagittarians might experience sudden bursts of anger or frustration. Because they speak directly and dislike feeling trapped, they can become annoyed if they think someone is limiting them, being unfair, or dismissing their ideas. During these moments, their anger might appear suddenly. They might raise their voice or stomp away. However, this anger often fades as fast as it arrived. Once they have had a moment to cool down, they might say, "I am sorry about that. I felt upset, but I am okay now."

This quick recovery can be refreshing, because they do not hold onto grudges for long. They might forgive a friend or family member soon after a disagreement. The catch is that they can leave others feeling startled, wondering how to handle this abrupt mood change. Over time, learning to manage their initial flash of anger more gently helps them avoid hurting those around them.

Sensitivity to Harsh Criticism

Even though Sagittarians seem outwardly confident, they can be more sensitive than many people suspect. When someone criticizes them in a harsh way, they can feel wounded. They might react by trying to prove the other person wrong, or by avoiding the critic entirely. This sensitivity is tied to their strong desire to do well and their wish to be seen as capable.

They can handle thoughtful, fair feedback, especially if it comes from someone they trust. But if the criticism feels mean-spirited or unfair, they might feel personally attacked. In that case, learning how to separate honest feedback from nasty remarks is key. It helps them decide what to ignore and what to use for growth. This skill can keep them from taking every comment to heart.

Empathy for Others

While some might think that Sagittarians only focus on their own interests, many of them do possess empathy toward others. They can sense when a friend or family member feels down. Because of their upbeat nature, they often try to cheer up the person with kind words or a fun distraction. Their natural positivity can make them good listeners if they set aside time to truly focus on the other person's feelings.

One thing they might need to practice is letting others fully express sadness or grief without rushing them to feel better. Sagittarians might quickly say, "It will be okay, don't worry," but the person might need a moment to cry or vent. Allowing space for deeper emotional release shows mature empathy. It reminds others that the Sagittarius truly cares about their feelings, not just about fixing the situation right away.

Dealing With Fear and Anxiety

Because Sagittarius is often seen as brave and curious, one might think they do not feel fear. In reality, they can experience worry just like anyone else. However, they may try to hide it by focusing on something more positive or by distracting themselves with an exciting activity. If the worry is about something that will not go away—like a personal issue or a health concern—this approach might not solve the problem in the long term.

Over time, many Sagittarians realize that talking about fears can reduce their intensity. They might speak with a close friend, counselor, or trusted mentor. They also benefit from healthy outlets such as exercise, art, or writing. Rather than pushing fear away, facing it step by step can help them feel more in control. Once they see that facing fears does not weaken their bright spirit, they can handle anxiety in a balanced way.

Balancing Restless Feelings

Sagittarians often carry restless energy. While it can be fun and exciting, it might also create inner tension if they feel stuck or bored. These restless feelings can show up as impatience, fidgeting, or daydreaming. Emotionally, this can make them irritable if they have to wait too long. For instance, if they are stuck in a slow-moving line or forced to do a task that feels dull, they might grow frustrated.

Learning ways to channel this restless energy helps them avoid emotional outbursts. They might take short breaks to walk around, stretch, or do a quick, simple activity. Even small breaks can help them refocus. Once they know how to handle restlessness, they can use their high energy in positive ways rather than letting it spiral into negative emotions.

Expression Through Creative Outlets

Many Sagittarians find that creative activities provide a safe space for expressing feelings they cannot put into simple words. They might write short stories, sketch, play an instrument, or do other crafts. While they do not always see themselves as "artists," they often have vivid imaginations and a knack for producing creative ideas.

Through these projects, they can reflect on what they feel without having to say it outright. For example, if they feel lonely, they might write a poem about a person searching for a friend. If they feel frustrated, they might paint bold and strong colors. These creative outlets can help them process complex emotions in a gentle, constructive way.

Handling Guilt and Regret

Sagittarius folks usually act with good intentions. However, if they realize they have acted too quickly and caused harm, they can feel guilty. Maybe they said something blunt that hurt a friend, or they forgot an important favor they promised to do. When guilt hits, they might experience a heavy sense of regret.

One of the best ways for them to handle guilt is by apologizing promptly and trying to make things right. They might say, "I see what I did wrong. I'm sorry. How can I fix it?" This direct approach can clear the air. If they avoid the issue, it can cause the guilt to build up, creating inner conflict. Learning to own mistakes and move forward is a skill that helps them mature emotionally.

Self-Reflection and Personal Growth

For a Sagittarius, self-reflection might not come naturally at first. They tend to be forward-looking, which can keep them from pausing to examine their own emotional patterns. Yet, as they grow older, many Sagittarians realize the value of thinking about how they feel and why. Simple self-checks—like asking, "Why did that comment upset me so much?"—can reveal hidden fears or insecurities.

Once they identify these deeper feelings, they can work on them through honest conversations or quiet moments of reflection. This process can lead to healthier emotional habits. Over time, a Sagittarius who practices self-reflection might become very wise about their own emotional triggers and how to handle them.

Building Emotional Bridges

Sagittarians can build emotional bridges with people by being open-minded listeners. When they truly focus on another person's feelings, they show genuine care. This can lead to closer connections, because the other person feels safe sharing their own emotions. In return, the Sagittarius might also begin to trust that person with their own private thoughts.

This give-and-take creates a supportive environment. Rather than only talking about exciting topics, they can also discuss worries, hopes, and sadness. Building these emotional bridges lets the Sagittarius see they are not alone in their feelings. It also helps their friends or family feel valued. Through patience and practice, Sagittarians can become pillars of support for others, and vice versa.

Coping With Changes

Life is full of changes. Some are exciting, like discovering a new activity, while others can be tough, such as moving to a new neighborhood. Because Sagittarians thrive on fresh experiences, they might seem to handle certain changes well. However, changes that remove their sense of freedom or comfort can cause deep emotional stress. For example, if they have to follow strict rules in a new setting, they might feel anxious or trapped.

In such cases, it helps them to find small ways to keep their sense of personal space. Maybe they set aside a short time each day for something they enjoy. Or they form a plan (even a basic one) to adapt gradually. By focusing on small steps, they can reduce worry about the bigger shift. Accepting that not all changes are thrilling but can still bring lessons is a key part of emotional growth for Sagittarius.

Encouraging Emotional Openness in Groups

When Sagittarians interact with friends or groups, they can encourage a lighthearted mood that makes others feel comfortable. This can make it easier for group members to share their thoughts. For instance, if a group is discussing a serious project, the

Sagittarius might sprinkle in playful comments to ease tension. As a result, the group feels more at ease and might open up about their concerns or ideas.

However, the Sagittarius should watch for moments when the group needs a more serious tone. If someone is feeling deep sadness or frustration, the group might need a calm, steady approach. Reading the room is crucial. By balancing their usual bright style with empathy, Sagittarians can create a safe group atmosphere that supports honest conversations.

Finding Healthy Distractions

Everyone sometimes needs a break from heavy feelings. Sagittarius folks are experts at finding distractions, whether that is engaging in sports, playing games, or reading about an interesting topic. Healthy distractions can give them time to cool down and think more clearly about a situation before tackling it again.

But there is a difference between a short, healthy break and ignoring a serious problem altogether. If a Sagittarius always dodges the main issue, it might grow over time. They can try setting a limit, like telling themselves, "I'll take a fun break for an hour, then I'll return to think about my problem and talk with someone about it if needed." This method helps them enjoy the good side of distraction without neglecting real issues.

Respecting Others' Emotional Boundaries

Sagittarians like directness, so they might offer help even when someone is not ready to discuss their feelings. For example, if they see a friend looking sad, they might ask, "What's wrong? Talk to me," without realizing the friend might need more time. While their caring motive is genuine, not everyone will want to open up on the spot.

A gentle approach—saying something like, "I'm here if you want to share anything"—can be more supportive. It allows the other person to decide when they are ready to talk. Over time, a Sagittarius can learn to spot these boundaries and offer help in a way that matches the other person's comfort level.

Emotional Expression in Conflicts

When conflicts arise, emotional expression can be tricky. Sagittarians might feel a rush of anger or annoyance if they think someone is acting unfairly. They might speak plainly about what they find bothersome. While this honesty can help solve misunderstandings quickly, it can also lead to harsh words if not controlled.

A useful approach is for the Sagittarius to pause, take a deep breath, and think, "I need to explain my side calmly." Counting to a small number or stepping away for a minute can prevent a heated outburst. Then they can come back and say, "This situation upsets me because…" in a calmer tone. This helps both sides understand each other without unnecessary emotional harm.

The Role of Optimism

Optimism is one of the strong suits of Sagittarius. They often believe that things will turn out for the better. This can keep them from feeling hopeless, even in tough times. They might say, "There must be a solution to this," and keep searching until they find it. This positive mindset can be an emotional lifeline for both the Sagittarius and the people around them.

However, constant optimism can sometimes cause them to overlook genuine problems. For instance, if a friend keeps showing signs of serious distress, the Sagittarius might think, "They'll be fine; they just need to cheer up." Real emotional support can involve acknowledging the depth of the issue. Striking a balance between optimism and reality helps them be a better friend to others and kinder to themselves.

Handling Grief and Loss

Grief and loss are among the toughest emotional trials anyone can face. Sagittarians, with their strong dislike of feeling stuck in sadness, may try to move on quickly. They might throw themselves into activities or new interests. While staying active can be part of healing, they may discover that certain feelings linger if not properly addressed.

Talking with a trusted person, writing letters to process the loss, or seeking guidance from a professional can help. Accepting that grief is a process, not a quick fix, can be difficult for someone who prefers to look ahead. Yet, once they allow themselves to mourn, they often find they can keep their spirit alive while also honoring the pain they feel.

Confidence in Emotional Expression

Sagittarians often come across as confident in many areas of life, including sharing basic feelings like joy or excitement. Over time, as they gain experience, they can also become more confident in showing deeper emotions. They might learn that letting friends or loved ones see them sad, anxious, or uncertain does not make them weak. In fact, it can build trust and closeness.

This does not mean they must share every detail with everyone. Boundaries are important. But having a few close people with whom they can be fully honest can strengthen their sense of connection and self-acceptance. This emotional confidence usually grows as they figure out who is truly supportive in their lives.

Emotions and Self-Image

A Sagittarius might tie their self-image to how well they handle problems. They might think, "I should always be the upbeat one," or "I'm supposed to be the fun friend who never gets bogged down." This can lead them to hide moments of doubt or sadness, fearing it does not fit with their usual image.

Realizing that self-image can include many emotions is a key step in emotional development. They learn they can still be the bright, uplifting person while admitting that sometimes they need support. This broader view of themselves actually makes them more genuine in the eyes of others. Instead of feeling they must always be positive, they recognize that human emotions are wide-ranging, and it is okay to experience them all.

Developing Emotional Patience

Sagittarius people can feel impatient, especially if they want quick resolutions to emotional challenges. They might say, "Let's fix this now," but some feelings do not resolve instantly. Emotions like deep sadness, guilt, or forgiveness might require repeated discussions or reflections over days or weeks.

Emotional patience means accepting that healing or understanding can take time. Rather than trying to rush it, they can stay present and supportive. This can be hard for them at first, but it leads to deeper growth. By learning to live with some uncertainty or unfinished feelings, they become more resilient and kind to themselves.

Sharing Emotions Through Writing

Writing can be a powerful tool for Sagittarians who find it tough to talk face-to-face about intense feelings. They might keep a private diary or write letters to themselves. This lets them place their thoughts in front of them, making it easier to understand worries or wishes that swirl in their minds.

Even writing messages to a trusted friend can be easier than speaking out loud. In written form, they have time to choose words carefully and fully explain themselves. This process can bring clarity and emotional release. Later, if they feel comfortable, they can discuss these writings openly, turning private reflection into shared support.

Learning from Emotional Setbacks

Everyone experiences emotional setbacks—times when we feel we have handled a situation poorly or let our temper flare. For a Sagittarius, these moments can be teaching points. Maybe they realize they jumped to conclusions about a friend's behavior. Perhaps they see they used humor at an inappropriate time. Instead of sinking into shame, a forward-thinking Sagittarius can ask, "What can I learn from this?"

They might write down a brief note about what happened and how they could handle it differently next time. For instance, "Next time I'm upset, I'll wait five minutes before speaking." Over time, these small lessons add up, helping them build healthier emotional patterns. Through this approach, they use mistakes as fuel for improvement.

CHAPTER 6: SAGITTARIUS IN LOVE

Love can be an exciting topic, especially for a sign known for openness and positive thinking. Sagittarius individuals have a special style when it comes to romance. They often love the idea of connecting deeply but can also feel uneasy if a relationship becomes too restrictive. This chapter focuses on how Sagittarians handle affection, attraction, commitment, and the natural ups and downs that can appear in romantic relationships. We will present fresh details not covered in prior chapters, keeping the discussion focused on love and the unique qualities of Sagittarius in this area.

Initial Attraction

Sagittarians are often drawn to people with bright minds or interesting perspectives. They may notice someone who can engage in thoughtful conversations, who has an upbeat sense of humor, or who carries a free spirit. Intellectual sparks and friendly curiosity often light the first spark of attraction for a Sagittarius.

This does not mean they only like people who share all the same views. Sometimes, they are intrigued by someone who thinks very differently, as long as that person is open to talking about new ideas. The main point is that they appreciate learning from a potential partner. If they feel mentally or emotionally stuck with someone, they might lose interest quickly.

The Flirting Style of Sagittarius

When it comes to flirting, Sagittarians can be playful and direct. They might tease a bit, ask many questions, or share funny stories to break the ice. Their bright energy can make them quite charming. Rather than using fancy words, they might keep it casual and friendly, focusing on genuine laughter and lighthearted banter.

Sometimes, they may flirt without meaning to, simply because they enjoy friendly chats. This can create confusion if the other person takes their words as romantic interest when the Sagittarius was only being sociable. Over time, they usually learn to be clearer about their feelings to avoid misunderstandings. Still, their warm and open manner often makes them well-liked in social circles.

Openness vs. Fear of Restriction

Sagittarius individuals love sharing time and energy with a partner, but they can also become uneasy if the relationship feels too confined. They want closeness, yet they also need personal space. For instance, they might be happy spending a whole day together, but they might also want time alone to pursue their own interests.

This balancing act can be puzzling to partners who expect constant togetherness. A Sagittarius does not usually thrive if someone tries to control their schedule or limit their friendships. They want a partner who understands that freedom is part of their personality. When they feel respected and trusted, they are more than willing to show loyalty in return.

Adventurous Dates and Shared Activities

Though we avoid certain terms, it is fair to say that Sagittarians enjoy fun and active ways of spending time with a loved one. They might love visiting interesting places, trying out a new sport, or exploring safe outdoor areas. Shared activities that bring excitement often deepen the bond, because Sagittarians value experiences that create lasting memories.

However, not all their time must be high-energy. They can also share quiet moments at home, cooking a simple meal or playing a card game. The key is that they do not want to get stuck in a repetitive cycle. Introducing small variations in shared activities can keep the spark alive for them.

Communication in a Sagittarius Relationship

Communication is central to any successful relationship. A Sagittarius, known for directness, usually prefers open and honest talks. They tend to say what they think, which can be refreshing but might also sound abrupt if they are not careful. For instance, if they see a problem, they might announce it plainly, without sugarcoating.

Partners who appreciate clarity often find this style helpful. But for those sensitive to blunt words, it might be a source of friction. Over time, a Sagittarius can learn to keep their frankness but add empathy in their tone. Simple phrases like, "This is how I see it, but I want to hear your side," can help keep communication respectful and balanced.

Emotional Sharing and Vulnerability

While Sagittarians can be open about many topics, they might feel hesitant when it comes to deeper emotional worries. They prefer to keep things light and positive, which can make them slow to reveal sadness, fear, or insecurities. A partner might sense that something is bothering them, yet the Sagittarius might joke it away.

Building mutual trust is key. Once they feel that their partner truly respects and understands them, a Sagittarius is more willing to share deeper feelings. It can be a gradual process, but each step of open sharing often brings them closer. Partners who offer patience and a safe space for honesty usually see the more hidden sides of the Sagittarius spirit.

Handling Conflict in a Romantic Setting

No relationship is free of conflict. When disagreements arise, Sagittarians often want to address them openly. They dislike feeling tension or pretending nothing is wrong. This can be good, as it prevents issues from festering. However, if anger flares up, they may speak too bluntly, hurting their partner's feelings in the process.

A helpful method is for them to pause and consider how to phrase their concerns. Instead of accusing, they can share personal feelings: "I feel upset when…" or "It worries me that…" This approach reduces defensiveness and encourages real understanding. Once the problem is on the table, Sagittarians tend to want a quick resolution. They also move on from fights fairly fast, provided both sides feel heard.

The Need for Mental Stimulation

Long-term relationships with Sagittarians often need some form of mental stimulation. They might enjoy discussing books, news, or interesting topics. If they feel bored, they can drift away emotionally. It is not that they require constant chatter; rather, they want to know their partner shares at least some curiosity about life.

Partners who engage with them in thoughtful discussions often strengthen the bond. Each person might learn something from the other's perspective. For instance, if the Sagittarius has a hobby like astronomy, the partner might join them in looking at the stars, or at least listen to them talk about it. These shared interests and talks nurture closeness.

Loyalty and Trust

Sagittarians can be very loyal if they genuinely care for their partner. They do not usually see love as a game and dislike lying or sneaking around. When they are committed, they expect the same level of honesty in return. A partner who breaks their trust may find it difficult to regain.

However, loyalty does not mean they will give up their personal independence. For them, a healthy relationship is one where both people can be faithful while still having their own identities. They want the freedom to see friends and follow their interests without suspicion. When trust is strong on both sides, they can be incredibly devoted and caring partners.

Gift-Giving and Thoughtful Gestures

When Sagittarians want to show affection, they often do so through surprises or thoughtful gestures. They might buy something quirky or meaningful that relates to an inside joke. Or they might plan a day out doing something they know their partner loves. These gestures are usually spontaneous, reflecting their bright spirit.

They can sometimes forget important dates if they are not careful. If they feel forced to make a grand gesture on a certain day, it might not come naturally. However, their genuine warmth can show up in everyday acts, like sending a funny message or doing a small favor to brighten the partner's day.

Respecting Personal Space in a Relationship

One of the biggest tests for a Sagittarius in love is balancing closeness with personal space. They want to feel free to explore their own hobbies, meet new people, or just have quiet alone time. A partner who becomes too clingy or suspicious can make them feel suffocated.

This does not mean Sagittarius wants to be distant. Rather, they thrive in a partnership where trust and independence go hand in hand. If they know they can pursue their interests without being questioned, they often return that same trust. In fact, giving them room to breathe can make them even more affectionate and present when they do spend time with their partner.

Talking About the Future

At some point, most couples discuss the future. Sagittarians might have a mix of excitement and caution in these talks. They can be open to the idea of long-term plans, but they also worry about losing their sense of independence. The idea of setting everything in stone might make them uneasy.

A balanced approach works best. Rather than forcing them to commit to every detail right away, gentle steps can help. For example, they might agree on shared goals but leave space for individual growth. If the partner remains flexible and supportive, the Sagittarius will likely embrace the idea of building a meaningful future together.

Dealing With Jealousy

Sagittarius is not usually a sign that struggles with jealousy. They tend to believe in freedom and might expect the same from their partner. However, if they feel their partner is hiding something or being dishonest, they can become upset. A jealous Sagittarius might react by withdrawing or confronting the issue directly.

On the partner's side, it helps to offer clear reassurance. Because Sagittarians value honesty, calmly explaining the situation and clarifying misunderstandings can resolve tension. Over time, establishing open communication and respecting boundaries reduces jealousy. A Sagittarius who feels secure rarely sees a need to worry over small matters.

Emotional Support in Tough Times

When a Sagittarius partner faces personal hardship, they might try to keep up a cheerful front. However, if the struggle is deep, they need a loving partner who can listen without pushing them to "just be happy." Being present, offering understanding, and gently urging them to talk can help them open up.

In return, a Sagittarius can provide uplifting support when a partner is down. They might share encouraging words, small gifts, or silly distractions to ease tension. The main point is balance. Both partners need to feel safe expressing real emotions. If a Sagittarius sees that their partner respects and acknowledges these feelings, they will do the same in return, creating a supportive bond.

Handling Long-Distance or Busy Times

Because Sagittarians value independence, they can handle periods of physical distance if both people are clear about expectations. For example, if one partner has to travel for work, the Sagittarius might use that time to follow personal interests, staying in contact through calls or texts. They do not like to feel restricted, so a balanced sense of freedom keeps them engaged.

However, they also appreciate consistent communication. Even though they can handle time apart, they do not want to be forgotten. A quick message or sharing a day's highlights can maintain emotional closeness. If the distance becomes so great that communication fails, they might start to feel disconnected. Finding a middle ground—enough independence but also regular updates—helps keep their love strong even across miles.

Romantic Surprises

Sagittarians often like to keep things interesting in a relationship. They may plan small surprises, like leaving a funny note somewhere or taking their partner to a new hangout spot. These spontaneous acts reflect their creative side and can spark shared happiness.

Sometimes, though, a Sagittarius might forget that not everyone loves surprises. A partner who prefers routines might feel uneasy if plans change suddenly. To avoid stress, a Sagittarius can learn to check in with their partner first, or at least drop hints. Even a little heads-up can make the surprise more fun and less startling.

Conflict Between Love and Freedom

Now and then, a Sagittarius might feel torn between wanting to deepen the relationship and wanting to keep exploring life on their own terms. They might worry that committing further means giving up personal freedoms. For them, it helps to recognize that healthy relationships do not need to limit personal growth. In fact, a good partner can support and encourage their wide-ranging interests.

Talking openly about these fears can prevent misunderstandings. If they assume that commitment always equals feeling trapped, they might push away a partner who could be very compatible. A partner who can say, "I respect your need for personal time, and I want to share some experiences together," can ease these fears. Over time, the Sagittarius sees that togetherness does not mean losing individuality.

Maintaining Positivity Through Challenges

When challenges arise, Sagittarians tend to look for solutions. In love, this can be helpful because they do not easily give up on the relationship. They might say, "Okay, let's figure out how to fix this problem." However, if they feel the same problems keep repeating with no real effort from the other side, they might lose patience.

Their partner can help by showing a genuine willingness to work things out. Shared brainstorming, honest talks, and small changes in behavior can keep the Sagittarius hopeful. If they see forward movement, they remain motivated. If they see no progress, they might eventually decide it is time to step back. They do not enjoy being stuck in a cycle of negativity.

Creative Ways of Expressing Affection

Sagittarius partners often show affection in ways that match their lively personalities. Instead of traditional gifts, they might create something unique that reflects an inside joke or a shared interest. Or they might plan a special outing that taps into their partner's favorite pastime. These acts remind the partner that the Sagittarius pays attention and genuinely wants to bring joy.

They can also be affectionate through words, leaving uplifting notes or sending spontaneous messages. It might not always be a flowery love letter; it could be a playful poem or a funny rhyme. However, some partners might crave more traditional romance. A Sagittarius who notices this could learn to add small romantic details like quiet evenings, heartfelt letters, or gentle moments that show tenderness.

Respecting a Partner's Emotional Style

Different people express love in different ways. A Sagittarius might be more playful and less inclined to sit and talk about feelings for hours. If they have a partner who needs deeper emotional discussions, conflict can arise if the Sagittarius seems to avoid serious talks. On the other hand, if the partner is also easygoing, they might blend well from the start.

In either case, respect is vital. A Sagittarius can learn to be patient during emotional talks, offering more than quick jokes. Meanwhile, the partner can accept that the Sagittarius might also show love through actions or fun events, not just long, intense talks. By meeting in the middle, they build a balanced emotional environment that fits both personalities.

Breaking Up or Parting Ways

Not all relationships last forever. If a breakup occurs, a Sagittarius might handle it with openness, wanting to talk things through. They might say, "We had great times, but we need to move on," hoping to leave on good terms. Because they prefer honesty, they might be direct about the reasons.

Still, parting ways can be painful, even if they try to keep a bright outlook. They might grieve the end of the connection but also lean on their optimism to imagine better days ahead. In some cases, they might wish to remain friends if the split was not too hurtful. However, they respect it if the other person needs space. Over time, they usually move forward, carrying lessons that shape their future approach to love.

Growth Over Time

Sagittarians in love do not remain the same forever. Over the years, they can become more open to deeper commitments, especially if they find a partner who supports their growth and respects their need for some independence. They might realize that sharing a life with someone does not mean losing their identity, but rather expanding it.

Likewise, a Sagittarius who once avoided serious topics might learn to handle them more gracefully. They might find that being emotionally vulnerable can lead to a stronger bond. By blending their natural cheer with deeper connection, they become loving partners who still maintain their spark.

Tips for Partners of Sagittarius

For someone dating or married to a Sagittarius, here are some helpful points to remember:

Stay Curious: A Sagittarius appreciates a partner who is interested in exploring topics or ideas together.

Support Independence: Show trust by letting them have personal interests, time with friends, and space to think.

Celebrate Small Wins: Give genuine praise or happiness when they share good news or reach a goal.

Be Ready for Change: They do not like to get stuck in a boring pattern. Suggest small twists or new experiences now and then.

Encourage Honest Talk: They do not mind discussing problems if the tone is fair. Try to speak calmly about issues.

Accept Their Style of Affection: Recognize that their way of showing love might be through jokes, playful surprises, or thoughtful acts, rather than grand romantic speeches.

Using these tips, partners can create a safe, warm environment in which Sagittarius individuals can thrive.

When Sagittarius is Truly in Love

When a Sagittarius truly falls in love, they show a remarkable level of devotion. Despite their fears about losing freedom, they can devote themselves to the partner's well-being. They might go out of their way to help or surprise their loved one, trying to share life's joys and challenges together.

It is not that they lose their sense of adventure; rather, they integrate their partner into that lively spirit. They might say, "Let's face these challenges together," or "I want to share my ideas with you." This sense of partnership can be very fulfilling for both sides. The Sagittarius feels they have someone who appreciates their spark while also providing stability when needed.

CHAPTER 7: WORK & CAREER

Sagittarius individuals bring a unique spark to their work and career paths. They are often driven by new ideas, open thinking, and a desire for independence. However, these same traits can present hurdles if they do not learn how to manage daily tasks, team dynamics, and workplace responsibilities. In this chapter, we will look at how Sagittarians typically behave in professional settings, what work styles suit them best, and how they might grow into their full potential. We will avoid repeating earlier content and concentrate on fresh insights about their attitude toward jobs and long-term goals.

Approach to Work

Sagittarians usually approach work with enthusiasm, especially if the job involves creativity or learning. They prefer roles that keep them interested. If a task feels repetitive, they may grow bored and start looking for a change. This can show up as job-hopping or taking on many small gigs rather than settling into one long-term position right away. While some might see this as unfocused, it can also mean that Sagittarians are searching for the best fit for their skills and interests.

If their job includes variety, chances to brainstorm, and room to experiment, they are more likely to stay interested. Sagittarians also appreciate workplaces that let them share thoughts openly. In many cases, a manager who allows them to propose fresh ideas and work without overly rigid rules can get the best out of a Sagittarius employee.

Searching for a Good Fit

When seeking a new position, Sagittarians often scan for key signals: is this role going to provide intellectual growth, or will it feel stifling? They might read job descriptions that promise flexible tasks, creative input, or the chance to talk to people from different backgrounds. They can be particularly attracted to positions tied to teaching, writing, public speaking, research, or anything that expands their mental horizons.

During interviews, Sagittarians usually come across as bright and confident. They often speak frankly and can hold a conversation with ease. However, they may need to watch out for being too informal. An interviewer might appreciate their sincerity, but also want to see that they can handle traditional workplace norms. Striking a balance between friendly chat and professional answers is key to making a good impression.

Workplace Conduct and Communication

In a professional setting, Sagittarians typically communicate in a direct and open way. They feel comfortable sharing opinions, which can be valuable in group discussions. If a project needs fresh angles, a Sagittarius might raise points that others have not considered. This directness usually helps the team, but it can also be a double-edged sword if they speak bluntly about sensitive subjects. Coworkers who are not used to frank feedback may take offense if they feel the Sagittarius is being too critical.

As they adapt to the professional environment, Sagittarians learn to read social cues and present ideas with a gentle approach. For example, instead of saying, "This plan is flawed," they might say, "Here's a different suggestion that could be helpful." With tact, they can blend their honesty with respect, forming strong relationships at work.

Independence and the Need for Autonomy

One of the most common things Sagittarians seek in any job is some level of autonomy. They do not enjoy being micromanaged. If a manager checks on them every few minutes or imposes very strict methods, they might feel frustrated and lose motivation. On the other hand, if they have the freedom to plan their own tasks or explore new approaches, their creativity and positivity can shine.

Team leaders who recognize this need can grant Sagittarians a degree of independence while still providing enough structure to ensure projects get done. This balance can work well, as Sagittarians will usually respect guidelines if they understand the reasons behind them. Giving them room to make some decisions on their own fosters better productivity and a happier mindset.

Handling Routine Tasks

While Sagittarians excel in roles that are varied, they often run into difficulty with tasks that require long-term repetition. If a job involves filling in the same forms daily or following the same procedure without change, their energy can fade. They might even procrastinate to avoid monotony. This can cause problems if their role demands a certain level of consistency.

To handle this, Sagittarians can try to see the bigger purpose behind repetitive tasks. They might tell themselves: "This routine job enables me to gain a steady income so I can focus on more interesting duties later." Or they might look for small ways to improve the process, bringing fresh ideas to streamline the workflow. By reframing the task or making small changes, they can keep their motivation alive.

Dealing with Coworkers and Team Projects

In team settings, Sagittarians often bring bright energy and a willingness to communicate. They might be the ones brainstorming big ideas at the start, encouraging others with their enthusiasm. However, they might lose interest once the project moves into fine details. This can cause tension if teammates feel the Sagittarius is quick to propose plans but slow to do the daily follow-up.

Learning to pace themselves can help. If they commit to a shared effort, they should remember to follow through on every step, not just the fun parts. They can also delegate tasks wisely, focusing on the areas where their skills shine and letting colleagues handle different parts. Good teamwork involves patience, mutual support, and finishing tasks fully, even if the tasks are not always the most exciting.

Leadership Style

Sagittarius individuals can be strong leaders if they learn to manage their team's varied needs. Their warm, open manner often motivates group members. They are the kind of leaders who might say, "Feel free to share any idea," and mean it. This makes many people feel comfortable speaking up. Sagittarians also like to see their team members develop new abilities over time.

Still, as leaders, they need to be aware that not everyone likes to be pushed into fresh concepts all at once. Some team members do better with familiar routines. A wise Sagittarius leader takes time to understand each person's style and gradually introduces new methods. While they trust their instincts, they can improve by seeking input from others, especially if the project needs thorough planning.

Career Fields That Suit Sagittarius

Because Sagittarians enjoy sharing knowledge, they may excel in fields such as education, training, writing, and publishing. Their curiosity can also guide them toward research, journalism, or roles that require understanding different opinions. If they like talking to people, sales or community outreach might be attractive. Travel-related careers can also be appealing, since many Sagittarians are interested in broadening their horizons (though they do not necessarily need to move around all the time—just knowing the job has variety can be enough).

They can also do well in creative roles like content creation or media production. The key is that they should avoid feeling boxed in. A job that offers mental stimulation, some independence, and room to grow is usually a better match for their nature.

Setting Goals and Keeping Focus

Sagittarians are often dreamers, thinking of big possibilities and imagining success down the road. However, the steps required to reach those goals can feel less appealing if they seem long or detailed. As a result, they might jump from one idea to another, hoping to find something that feels instantly fulfilling. This can lead to a pattern of incomplete projects or half-finished initiatives.

Learning to break down major goals into smaller tasks can help. For instance, if a Sagittarius wants to start a tutoring service, they might break it into steps: design lesson materials, find a location, reach out to potential students, set up a schedule, and so on. By handling each mini-step, they build momentum. This approach helps them see tangible progress, which keeps them motivated to push forward.

Coping with Criticism in the Workplace

Sagittarians can be sensitive to harsh feedback, especially if it feels personal. In a workplace review, if a manager points out something they need to improve, they might take it to heart more than they show. Their initial reaction might be to feel defensive or to argue. However, after some reflection, many Sagittarians will see the value in constructive guidance.

They can grow by asking clarifying questions. For example, "Can you show me an example of what you'd like me to do differently?" This approach turns criticism into a learning moment. Once they realize the feedback is about refining a process and not a personal attack, they can adapt quickly. Over time, a healthy response to feedback can make them stronger employees or leaders.

Stress and Time Management

Because Sagittarians like moving from idea to idea, time management can be tricky. They might forget deadlines if they are lost in brainstorming or exploring side tasks. This can cause avoidable stress. A helpful habit is to keep a clear schedule, perhaps using simple digital tools or a basic planner with alarms for important tasks. By checking tasks daily, they reduce the chance of missing deadlines.

Sagittarians also benefit from breaks during the day. If they work on a strict timeline, they can let themselves take short pauses to clear their mind. Stepping away for a few minutes can recharge their energy and restore focus. This helps them come back to tasks with fresh eyes, limiting mistakes caused by restlessness.

Adaptability in Changing Environments

Many modern workplaces go through changes, such as organizational shifts or new technology. Sagittarians often handle these shifts better than some other signs, because they do not mind switching up routines and testing different methods. They might even welcome the novelty, seeing it as a chance to try a fresh angle or learn a skill they did not have before.

However, they should make sure that constant changes do not distract them from finishing core responsibilities. It is one thing to adapt, but quite another to lose track of each project. Balancing openness to updates with the need for stability and completion is an important step. By doing so, Sagittarians can gain a reputation for being flexible but also dependable.

Long-Term Career Vision

At the start of their career, Sagittarians may jump around, trying to find the perfect role. But as they grow, many become more aware of what they truly want. Some might choose entrepreneurship, enjoying the control and freedom it provides. Others might become experts in a specific field, like research or academic roles, where they can keep learning.

The main turning point often comes when they realize they can combine their natural optimism with real planning. By deciding on a broader direction—such as becoming a top educator, a skilled consultant, or a creative project lead—they can channel their energy more effectively. This does not mean they become rigid; it simply means they have a target to aim for, which helps them stay committed.

Work Ethics and Values

Sagittarians usually show respect for fairness and honesty. They do not enjoy hidden schemes or underhanded moves in the workplace. If they sense shady behavior, they might speak up. This can be both good and challenging. Standing for what is right can improve company culture, but it might also lead to conflicts if the environment is not open to change.

They are also often generous with ideas, willing to share knowledge with colleagues. If someone asks for help, Sagittarians might pause their own tasks to assist, which can be a sign of a giving spirit. But they need to ensure they are not taken advantage of or overwhelmed by always saying yes. Setting boundaries on how much they can help allows them to maintain productivity.

Managing Boredom and Seeking Growth

A key challenge for Sagittarians is managing boredom. If they feel stuck in one role with no way to learn new skills, their motivation might plummet. They could start looking for a new job or become restless at the office, which can impact their performance. Ideally, they need ongoing learning or tasks that offer a bit of creative challenge.

They might talk to a supervisor about rotating tasks or taking on side projects that excite them. If this is not possible, they can look into short courses or workshops outside of work. Improving themselves helps them stay interested, and it can also give them an edge when they apply for higher-level positions later. By finding small ways to push themselves forward, they reduce the urge to abandon a role too soon.

Public Speaking and Presentation

Many Sagittarians are natural speakers who do well in front of a group. They can use humor, stories, and genuine enthusiasm to make a point. Because they usually have strong communication skills, jobs that involve speaking, teaching, or presenting can be a great match. They might run workshops, pitch projects to clients, or host online webinars.

However, they should remember the importance of preparation. While improvisation can be fun, a well-structured talk often has more impact. Gathering facts and outlining main points can help them speak with clarity, so they do not rely solely on their ability to "wing it." This balanced approach—mixing free expression with a solid structure—often wins over audiences.

Handling Deadlines and Pressure

At times, Sagittarians might push deadlines until the last moment, partly because they do not like rigid rules. But this can lead to last-minute stress and mistakes. To avoid this, they can practice breaking large deadlines into smaller, more manageable chunks. For example, if a big report is due in two weeks, they can set mini-deadlines for outlining, research, drafting, and editing. Each step can have its own small due date.

This method keeps them on track and reduces the risk of panic. By spreading out the tasks, they also give themselves enough time to polish the final product. Over time, this skill can turn a Sagittarius from a chronic procrastinator into a more reliable team member or leader.

Conflict Resolution at Work

In a fast-paced workplace, disagreements are common. Sagittarians, with their honest approach, may face conflicts if they speak too sharply or if they openly question rules. However, they can also be the ones to settle disputes, as they often aim for fairness. They might step in and say, "Let's hear both sides calmly." This can help coworkers feel that someone is looking out for a fair solution.

The main point for Sagittarians is to ensure they do not add to the conflict by becoming hotheaded. If they sense their own frustration rising, taking a brief pause to breathe can help. Then they can return with a calmer mindset, ready to address the problem. By practicing patience, they can build a reputation as someone who knows how to handle tense situations positively.

Mentoring and Guiding Others

Given their love for spreading knowledge, many Sagittarians are excellent mentors. They enjoy sharing tips, explaining concepts, or helping new hires settle in. This teaching spirit can shine in workplaces that reward employee growth. As mentors, Sagittarians can encourage others to ask questions and think broadly.

They should be sure to follow through if they promise help. Sometimes, a Sagittarius might volunteer to train someone but then get distracted by their own workload. By making a schedule (for example, setting aside an hour each week for guidance), they can provide steady support. This also helps them keep track of their own tasks without neglecting their mentees.

Balancing Work and Personal Life

Because Sagittarius individuals can pour a lot of energy into new projects, they might find themselves working long hours if they are truly inspired. On the other hand, if the job bores them, they might not give it their all. Finding balance is key. It helps if they plan personal time for relaxation, hobbies, or social events. This makes them feel refreshed, so they can return to work with a better attitude.

If a job becomes too demanding, they might grow resentful, feeling it steals all their freedom. Being honest about workloads and limits can prevent burnout. Talking with a manager or adjusting schedules might be necessary to stay healthy and happy. A balanced life ultimately allows Sagittarians to give their best at work without sacrificing their personal well-being.

Growing Professional Confidence

Sagittarians often have a natural self-assurance, but professional confidence might take longer to build. They can become uneasy if they are in a job that feels too big for their skill level. Yet, if they only pick tasks that are easy, they will not grow. The best scenario is to choose roles or projects that stretch their abilities slightly beyond what they already know.

By taking on mildly challenging tasks and seeking feedback, they can watch their skills improve step by step. Each success grows their professional confidence. Even when mistakes happen, they can view them as lessons. Over time, they gather enough experience to feel secure in their capabilities, without losing the willingness to learn and adapt.

Problem-Solving Strengths

Sagittarians often excel at seeing the broad picture when a team faces a complex issue. They can look past small details and notice patterns or possibilities that others might miss. This can be very useful in brainstorming sessions or strategic planning. They might propose solutions that sound bold, but sometimes boldness is exactly what a project needs.

However, they should remember to back their ideas with facts or practical steps. If they only provide a broad vision without explaining how to put it into action, coworkers might remain confused. By combining their natural creativity with a bit of planning, they can create robust solutions that truly help their team or company.

Workplace Challenges and How to Overcome Them

1. **Boredom:** As discussed, variety and learning help Sagittarians stay engaged.

2. **Procrastination:** Breaking tasks down and setting mini-deadlines can help.

3. **Over-scheduling:** Because Sagittarians want to try everything, they might overbook themselves. Learning to say no or to delegate is key.

4. **Impatience:** Deep breathing, short breaks, or even a quick walk can calm them during frustrating moments.

5. **Blunt Speech:** Pausing to consider word choices and tone keeps relationships friendly.

By handling these hurdles, they can reach success without compromising their natural energy or positivity.

Self-Employment and Entrepreneurship

Some Sagittarians find traditional jobs too restrictive and choose to start their own businesses. They might open an online store, offer freelance services, or create a platform to teach skills. This path allows them full control over how they work, which can be very appealing. They can set their own hours, pick projects that spark their interest, and pivot as needed.

However, running a business also involves repetitive tasks such as finances, marketing details, and paperwork. A Sagittarius can handle this by hiring or partnering with someone who loves handling details. That way, they stay focused on big-picture items, while their partner manages the day-to-day operations. With a good team, they can thrive in the self-employment world.

Conclusion of Work and Career

For Sagittarius individuals, work can be a place to explore, learn, and engage with interesting tasks. They usually prefer jobs that offer mental stimulation and a friendly environment. Their direct speech, open-mindedness, and generosity of ideas can make them valuable contributors. Yet, they also need to watch out for boredom, overcommitment, and forgetting about the finer details.

By practicing good time management, being patient with coworkers, and breaking down larger goals, Sagittarians can grow into impressive professionals or leaders. In the end, they might find long-term satisfaction in roles that let them blend their excitement for fresh concepts with the practical skills needed for success. If they manage to balance independence with teamwork, detail with big ideas, and honesty with respect, they can carve out a meaningful and rewarding career path.

CHAPTER 8: STRENGTHS & WEAKNESSES

Sagittarius people, like every zodiac sign, have a range of positive traits and areas that might cause them trouble. By recognizing both sides, they can make the best use of their positive points while managing or reducing the effects of the negative ones. This chapter will outline Sagittarius strengths and weaknesses in a way that does not repeat earlier chapters. We will focus on how these traits can show up in everyday life, rather than just describing them in vague terms.

Emphasis on Strengths and Weaknesses

Understanding one's own strengths and weaknesses is crucial for growth and self-awareness. Sagittarians who see their strong traits clearly can bring a spark to every setting—home, school, work, and friendships. At the same time, facing weaknesses gives them a chance to adapt and overcome hurdles that might block their progress.

This balanced view helps them accept themselves for who they are, rather than trying to ignore flaws or pretend they have no challenges. They can also use their strengths in thoughtful ways to help others. Let us explore these strengths and weaknesses in detail, keeping the information fresh and not repeating what was shared in earlier parts of this book.

Strength: Open-Mindedness

Many Sagittarians are open to new ideas and fresh perspectives. If someone presents a different angle or an unfamiliar topic, they are usually willing to listen, at least for a while. This quality can lead to interesting conversations and surprising discoveries. It helps them form friendships with people from various backgrounds. It also makes them lifelong learners who are not afraid to explore untested concepts.

Daily Impact:

- They might be the first to try a new type of food or watch a documentary on an unusual subject.

- They often invite friends to discuss contrasting opinions, showing curiosity rather than immediate dismissal.

Weakness: Inconsistency

While Sagittarians have strong interest in multiple topics, they can struggle with consistency. They might lose focus on a project once the initial thrill fades, hopping on to something else that looks more fun. This can result in many half-done tasks or big plans that never fully take shape. It can also frustrate people counting on them.

Daily Impact:

- They might be known among friends for constantly shifting hobbies.

- They could start a big craft or writing project and forget about it after a few days.

- People might learn to wait and see if the Sagittarius stays committed before fully joining in.

Strength: Natural Optimism

Sagittarians often have a bright outlook on life. They try to see solutions instead of focusing on obstacles. This positivity can spread to those around them. During stressful times, they might say something that lightens the mood or reminds everyone that there is a way forward. They can lift spirits in a way that feels genuine and supportive.

Daily Impact:

- They might encourage a friend who feels worried about a test, saying, "You've studied well, and you'll do fine."

- They could provide an upbeat viewpoint in a family discussion, turning a tense atmosphere into something more hopeful.

- They might inspire teammates at work by pointing out small wins.

Weakness: Tendency to Oversimplify

Because of their positive outlook, Sagittarians might overlook the deeper details of a problem. They might say, "It will work out," without fully considering the steps needed or the potential difficulties. This can be frustrating for people who want to plan carefully. It can also lead to mistakes if the Sagittarius jumps in without checking all angles.

Daily Impact:

- They might volunteer for a school committee but fail to notice the time or effort required.

- They could plan an event without thinking about logistics, such as location or budget.

- In serious matters, they might brush off warnings, saying, "Don't worry," when some caution is actually needed.

Strength: Honesty

Sagittarians generally prefer speaking the truth. They do not enjoy playing games or being vague when sharing opinions. This can build trust because people know that a Sagittarius friend or coworker is not likely to lie or hide important points. If you ask for a straightforward view, they will probably give it, which can cut through confusion.

Daily Impact:

- They might tell a sibling exactly what they think of a plan, good or bad.

- They give clear, direct responses when asked for advice.

- They rarely keep secrets about their own thoughts; if they feel strongly, they will say so.

Weakness: Bluntness Can Hurt Feelings

While honesty is valuable, Sagittarians can sometimes speak with a blunt tone that stings. They may not notice how words can sound harsh to someone who is more sensitive. This can lead to accidental hurts or arguments, especially if the other person was not ready for that level of frankness.

Daily Impact:

- A Sagittarius might criticize a friend's art project in front of a group, thinking they are just being helpful.

- They might correct someone's mistake in a direct manner, causing the person to feel embarrassed instead of guided.

- Friends or coworkers may learn to brace themselves before asking for an opinion.

Strength: Love of Freedom

Many Sagittarians deeply treasure their independence. They enjoy exploring fresh experiences, forming new connections, and embracing the unknown. This sense of freedom can make them fun companions, as they are open to last-minute plans or big changes. It also fosters creativity because they are not afraid to test different ways of doing things.

Daily Impact:

- They might suddenly decide to take a day trip to a nearby place they have never seen before.

- They could shift their bedroom furniture around on a whim, liking the feeling of a different setup.

- They might join a new social group just because it sparks their interest.

Weakness: Discomfort with Rules and Routines

While their need for freedom can be exciting, Sagittarians might resist rules, even when those rules are helpful. If a parent, teacher, or boss tries to enforce strict guidelines, they might feel restricted. This could result in conflicts or missed opportunities. Sometimes, ignoring routine tasks leads to trouble, like forgetting deadlines or skipping steps in a process.

Daily Impact:

- They might argue with a teacher about homework policies if they see them as too rigid.

- They could skip routine chores at home, causing frustration within the family.

- In a workplace, they might clash with a manager who wants them to follow a set procedure every day.

Strength: Generosity and Warmth

Sagittarians often have big hearts. They like to help, share, and offer support to friends and loved ones. If someone is facing a hard time, a Sagittarius might be the first to organize a small show of support or give what they can. This warm spirit can make others feel cared for and important.

Daily Impact:

- They might share resources freely, whether that is giving away extra items or lending money to a friend in need.

- They invite new classmates or coworkers to join social activities, making them feel welcome.

- They sometimes offer to teach a skill or explain a concept just because they see someone struggling.

Weakness: Overcommitting to Others

Because they like to be helpful, Sagittarians can promise more than they can deliver. They might say, "Yes, I'll help with that event," but forget they also promised to complete a work task and have a family obligation the same evening. This leads to stress, late hours, and possibly disappointing results. Overcommitting can also drain them, making them feel stretched too thin.

Daily Impact:

- They might try to attend two parties on the same night, rushing between them and barely enjoying either.

- They may tell friends they can help with homework while also having a personal project due.

- Family members might notice they often say, "I'll be there," only to cancel because they realize they have double-booked themselves.

Strength: Ability to Inspire Others

Sagittarians bring an uplifting tone to gatherings. Their eagerness for fresh experiences and big ideas can inspire those around them to aim higher. They can spark excitement in group projects, social events, or creative tasks. When they talk about possibilities, they often sound convincing, encouraging others to give it a try.

Daily Impact:

- They might pep up a study group with words like, "This subject can be interesting if we look at it from another angle!"

- They could motivate a friend to pursue an artistic dream by showing genuine enthusiasm.

- In a sports team, they might rally players with an upbeat speech or friendly cheers.

Weakness: Difficulty Accepting Limitations

Sometimes, the positive spirit of a Sagittarius leads them to think everything can be solved with enough hope. While optimism is wonderful, it can become unrealistic if they refuse to acknowledge real-world constraints. This might cause them to be blind to financial limits, time limits, or other practical factors. They might push forward without the necessary planning and then feel disappointed when obstacles appear.

Daily Impact:

- They might plan a major personal project without checking if they have the needed resources.

- In a group assignment, they could promise big outcomes but ignore the tight deadline.

- They may advise friends to take a big risk without helping them prepare for any downside.

Strength: Ability to Bounce Back

Even when Sagittarians face failures, they often recover quickly. They usually do not stay discouraged for long. They tend to believe that tomorrow brings another chance. This can be a powerful skill, as they remain hopeful in tough times. Their resilience helps them try again rather than giving up.

Daily Impact:

- After a poor grade on a test, they might say, "I'll study differently next time," and feel genuinely ready to do better.

- If a business idea does not work out, they might brainstorm fresh approaches instead of quitting.

- They do not dwell too long on mistakes but prefer to view them as stepping stones.

Weakness: Overconfidence

The same energy that helps them bounce back can turn into overconfidence if they are not careful. They might dismiss the need to prepare because they think their natural charm or quick thinking will see them through. Over time, this can cause them to miss key details or fail to study important information.

Daily Impact:

- They might show up to a presentation with minimal preparation, relying on improvisation.

- In a sports setting, they might skip practice, believing their natural talent is enough.

- They could accept tasks without reading instructions, convinced they can figure it out later.

Strength: Sense of Humor

Sagittarius individuals usually have a good sense of humor. They see something funny in everyday happenings and can turn a dull moment into a round of laughter. This lighthearted side helps relieve tension, making them enjoyable company in social or family circles.

Daily Impact:

- They might make a quick joke during a quiet meeting, breaking the ice and helping everyone relax.

- With friends, they often come up with puns or silly comments that keep the mood bright.

- They can handle minor setbacks by laughing them off, which keeps stress from building up.

Weakness: Unintentionally Avoiding Seriousness

Their playful side can sometimes prevent them from addressing pressing matters. If something serious needs careful thought, they may try to gloss over it with humor. While laughter is healthy, it can become a block if it stops them from dealing with real problems.

Daily Impact:

- They might joke around when a loved one tries to discuss an emotional topic.

- They could ignore a warning sign about their own health or finances, making light of the situation instead.

- If conflict arises, they might try to use humor to dodge a needed talk, causing the issue to linger.

Strength: Cultural Appreciation

Sagittarians frequently enjoy exploring different cultures, viewpoints, and lifestyles. They often do not limit themselves to what they are used to. This can lead to them studying new languages, cooking dishes from around the world, or reading books that broaden their perspective.

Daily Impact:

- They might learn common phrases in a foreign language just for fun.

- They could try recipes from other countries, inviting friends to taste them.

- In discussions about global events, they offer open-minded ideas and willingness to learn.

Weakness: Restlessness

Because they love variety, Sagittarians can become restless if stuck in the same space or dealing with the same routines for too long. This might lead to them rushing into changes without thinking them through. They could move homes, change jobs, or end relationships quickly because they feel bored.

Daily Impact:

- They might start rearranging everything in a room simply because they feel edgy.

- At work, they could switch roles abruptly when they sense monotony, sometimes losing progress in the process.

- Family members might describe them as "always on the move," never content for too long in one spot.

Strength: Willingness to Learn from Mistakes

Despite occasional overconfidence, many Sagittarians do reflect on errors once they recognize them. They might say, "I see where I messed up," and adjust their behavior. They do not typically dwell on guilt or regrets. Instead, they treat mistakes as stepping stones that help them grow.

Daily Impact:

- After getting negative feedback at work, they might say, "Next time, I'll approach this differently."

- A failed attempt at a new hobby could lead them to take lessons or watch tutorials to improve.

- They might apologize to friends if they realize they were too blunt, then make an effort to speak more kindly.

Weakness: Lack of Detail Orientation

Sagittarians often prefer broad concepts over small details. This can cause them to overlook crucial information. If they skip reading instructions or forget important steps, it leads to errors that could have been avoided. While their big-picture thinking is valuable, ignoring details can create stumbling blocks.

Daily Impact:

- They might put together a piece of furniture incorrectly because they skipped the guide.

- In a group project, they could forget to format a document properly, causing delays.

- They may fail to notice an important change in a schedule or plan, disrupting others.

Strength: Desire to Lift Others Up

Sagittarians like to see people happy and thriving. They might share motivational phrases or give heartfelt encouragement. This caring side shows itself when a friend or family member needs an extra push or comforting words. Sagittarians can be very supportive, urging others to believe in themselves.

Daily Impact:

- They might send cheerful messages to a friend before a big exam.

- They could praise a coworker's improvement, highlighting small wins that might otherwise go unnoticed.

- They may volunteer to help in community events aimed at boosting spirits or providing resources to those in need.

Weakness: Ignoring Personal Limits

In their wish to do everything—help friends, start new tasks, engage in fun outings—Sagittarians can ignore their own limits. They might not notice they are tired or stressed until it hits them all at once. This can lead to burnout or sudden emotional lows, as they have not paced themselves properly.

Daily Impact:

- They might agree to lead a group meeting on the same weekend they planned a family reunion, stretching themselves too thin.

- They could stay up late multiple nights in a row, trying to finish tasks, and then crash with exhaustion.

- They may say yes to every request from friends, forgetting they also need downtime.

Balancing Strengths and Weaknesses

To make the most of their qualities, Sagittarians can try pairing a strong trait with a practical habit that keeps weaknesses in check. For example, pairing optimism (a strength) with thorough planning can prevent them from oversimplifying tasks. Or pairing generosity (a strength) with the ability to say no can prevent them from overcommitting.

Possible Strategies:

1. **Set Realistic Goals:** When they feel inspired by a big idea, they can write smaller, practical steps. This channels optimism without ignoring real limits.

2. **Practice Self-Reflection:** They can take a moment each day to think about what went well and what went wrong, learning from both.

3. **Seek Feedback:** Let friends, coworkers, or family members point out details or issues they might have missed. This covers the weak side of detail orientation.

4. **Use Friendly Communication:** They can keep their honesty but soften the edges with kindness, ensuring they do not hurt others by being blunt.

Conclusion of Strengths and Weaknesses

Sagittarius individuals have a rich mix of positive traits—openness, honesty, warmth, humor, and a sense of possibility. These qualities can make them uplifting companions, adventurous learners, and supportive leaders. At the same time, their weaknesses—bluntness, restlessness, overconfidence, and difficulty with routine—can cause real hurdles if not recognized.

By actively working on these weaker points, they can grow into more balanced and steady versions of themselves. This does not mean they must become completely different; rather, they can shape their raw qualities so that others benefit from their strengths without getting caught in the pitfalls of their weaknesses. With awareness and effort, Sagittarians can shine brightly and form strong, lasting bonds at home, at school, in friendships, and at work. Their inherent positivity, paired with a practical approach to their weaker spots, can lead to a well-rounded, fulfilling life that reflects the best of what this star sign has to offer.

CHAPTER 9: COMMUNICATION STYLE

Sagittarius individuals often have a distinct way of communicating with the world around them. They tend to be lively, upbeat, and eager to share thoughts. However, there is more to their communication style than simply being cheerful or loud. Many Sagittarians have layers to the way they speak, listen, and connect with others, depending on the setting and who they are talking to. This chapter explores different parts of Sagittarius communication, from their openness to their potential bluntness, and offers ideas on how they can refine this style. We will keep the discussion fresh, focusing on how Sagittarians get their messages across and how they can handle different social settings without going over points already covered.

Speaking With Energy

One of the first things people notice about Sagittarius folks is that they often have a lively spark when they talk. They might speak with a certain rhythm or a noticeable excitement. Their words can come out quickly if they are excited about a topic. When a Sagittarius is in a good mood and wants to share an idea, it can feel like a bright burst of energy in the conversation.

This liveliness can be fun for listeners. They might smile because the Sagittarius person's excitement is contagious. However, it can also be a bit much for quieter or more reserved people, who might need a calmer pace to keep up. Learning to notice when others look overwhelmed can help a Sagittarius slow down or ask, "Is this making sense so far?" This way, they ensure everyone stays on the same page.

Desire for Real Dialogue

Sagittarians usually do not like small talk for too long. They might start with a quick greeting or a fun remark, but soon, they want to shift to something more meaningful, funny, or interesting. They can move the conversation toward topics that spark thoughts or laughter, rather than just talking about the weather. This love of genuine dialogue can lead them to ask questions like, "What do you think about this idea?" or "Have you noticed something interesting about that?"

While this is a good trait—it keeps chats engaging—Sagittarians should remember that not everyone is ready to go deep right away. Some people appreciate a slower entry into meaningful topics. Taking a moment to check if the other person is comfortable can prevent a situation where one party feels rushed into big discussions.

Openness and Honesty

Many Sagittarians are known for speaking plainly. They might tell you exactly what is on their mind, even if it sounds abrupt. On the positive side, this honesty helps others trust them. People know a Sagittarius is less likely to hide opinions or use tricky words. In group discussions, this can be refreshing. If a team needs feedback on a new plan, the Sagittarius member might give a clear viewpoint that pushes the group to think carefully.

On the other hand, being too honest can sometimes create awkward moments. For example, if someone asks for an opinion on a new outfit, the Sagittarius might say, "I don't like it at all," without softening the words. The friend might feel offended or hurt.

Learning to add kind phrasing—such as, "It's not my style, but if you like it, that's okay"—can make honesty easier for others to accept. By blending openness with kindness, Sagittarians can stay true to themselves while also respecting people's feelings.

Balancing Humor

Sagittarians often have a good sense of humor that shows up in their conversations. They might crack jokes, share funny stories, or tease friends in a lighthearted way. This humor can lift the mood and make people around them feel at ease. It helps them connect quickly, because laughter often brings people closer.

However, humor can become a stumbling block if it pops up at the wrong time. If someone is discussing a heavy concern—like an emotional problem or a big worry—and the Sagittarius instantly jokes, it might seem dismissive. Timing is key. Sagittarians who learn when to be funny and when to stay serious can use their humor as a powerful way to bond, rather than a tool that sidesteps genuine problems. Asking themselves, "Is this a good time to joke?" can help keep conversations respectful.

Nonverbal Signals

Communication is not just words. Nonverbal signals—like facial expressions, gestures, and posture—also matter. Sagittarians who feel excited might lean forward, grin widely, or wave their hands around as they speak. Their faces often reveal how they feel in the moment. This can make them easy to read, and it can also help others sense that their enthusiasm is real.

But if a Sagittarius is upset or impatient, they might roll their eyes or tap their foot without realizing it. These small actions can send a strong message that they disagree or want the conversation to hurry up. Becoming aware of these signals can help a Sagittarius avoid accidentally showing disrespect or impatience. If they notice themselves rolling their eyes, they can try taking a breath and patiently returning to the conversation. Small changes in nonverbal cues can improve their overall communication.

Adjusting to Different Audiences

A Sagittarius might speak one way with close friends, another way with teachers or bosses, and a different way with younger kids. This does not mean they are being fake; it simply means they adapt to what each situation needs. For example, with good friends, they might use more jokes and casual language. With a teacher, they might focus on polite, respectful phrasing and clearer organization of ideas.

Sometimes, Sagittarians forget to shift gears. If they talk to a teacher the same way they talk to a best friend, it might come off as too casual or even rude. Learning to adapt their style can save them from awkward mistakes. Practicing short polite phrases—like "Thank you for your help" or "I appreciate your feedback"—can show that they understand the basics of speaking to authority figures while staying genuine to who they are.

Listening Skills

Communication is not just about talking; it also involves listening closely to others. While Sagittarians can excel at sharing ideas, they might sometimes get so excited about their own thoughts that they jump in too soon. In group discussions or casual chats, they might cut someone off to add their own point, not noticing that the other person had not finished.

To improve listening, a Sagittarius can practice waiting a moment after someone finishes speaking before responding. A simple trick is to count one or two seconds in their head to ensure the other person is done. They can also nod or use small words like, "I see," or "Got it," to show they are following along. By doing this, they help the speaker feel respected and more open to hearing the Sagittarius's ideas in return.

Diplomacy in Conflict

Sagittarians are not always shy about disagreements. They might speak up if they think an idea is wrong or if they sense unfair behavior. This courage can be good, but it also requires diplomacy—knowing how to present disagreements calmly so that the discussion does not turn into a heated argument. Instead of saying, "That's a dumb idea," they might say, "I see your point, but here's a concern I have."

The goal is to keep the conversation respectful, even when strong opinions differ. It can help to start with something they do agree on before introducing the point of difference. For instance, "I agree that we need a better plan for our event, but I'm worried about the cost of this approach." This method helps the other person feel understood and less defensive.

Written Communication

While many Sagittarians prefer face-to-face chats (which allow for real-time exchange of ideas), written forms of communication—like emails, text messages, or letters—can be equally important. Some Sagittarians enjoy writing, especially if they have time to craft their thoughts carefully. Others might find it a bit slow because they like the fast pace of talking. Still, in school or work, they will often need to email teachers, managers, or classmates.

In written communication, it can help to be clear, direct, and polite. This is especially true in formal settings. Even if a Sagittarius has a light or funny style, they might need to adjust for certain audiences.

For example, emails to a boss or teacher should be spelled correctly, have polite greetings, and avoid too many slang words. On the other hand, friendly chats or text messages can be less formal. Learning the difference helps Sagittarians shine in all types of written communication.

Public Speaking

Because of their natural confidence and cheerful spirit, many Sagittarians are good at public speaking or presentations. They might enjoy addressing a classroom, leading a group discussion, or performing in front of an audience. Their energy can keep people engaged, and their honest way of speaking can feel relatable. However, there are a few things to watch for:

- **Preparation:** Even though they might enjoy winging it, having a clear outline or note cards can prevent stumbles or long pauses.

- **Staying on Topic:** Sagittarians might wander from the main subject if they get a sudden idea. Keeping an eye on the main points helps the audience follow along.

- **Friendly Tone:** Smiling and making eye contact can show warmth and openness, helping the audience feel connected.

With some practice, Sagittarians can become strong public speakers who use their natural flair to inform or entertain.

Handling Misunderstandings

In any conversation, misunderstandings can happen. A Sagittarius might say something jokingly, but the other person takes it seriously.

Or they might talk so fast that others miss the main idea. When these slip-ups occur, it is important to address them calmly:

1. **Check the Other Person's Feelings:** If someone seems upset or confused, a Sagittarius can ask, "Did what I say bother you?" This shows care.

2. **Explain Gently:** If it was a joke or a passing remark, they can say, "I didn't mean to upset you. Let me explain what I really meant."

3. **Listen to the Response:** Give the other person time to share their perspective. Sometimes, just letting them speak can clear the air quickly.

By being open to hearing feedback, a Sagittarius can maintain positive connections even when mix-ups occur.

Body Language Awareness

We talked about nonverbal signals earlier, but it is worth focusing on body language a bit more. Because Sagittarians can be restless, they might tap their feet, shift in their seat, or glance around the room. People might interpret this as boredom or impatience, even if the Sagittarius is actually just full of energy. Being mindful of these habits can prevent giving the wrong impression.

If a Sagittarius notices these restless habits in a serious or calm discussion, they can try small strategies, like clasping their hands in their lap or taking a slow breath before speaking. This can project steady attention, showing the speaker they have the Sagittarius's full focus.

Politeness and Respect

In formal or traditional environments, showing politeness matters a lot. Sagittarians sometimes skip formalities because they feel it's more authentic to be casual. But certain people or settings value politeness as a sign of respect. Simple habits—like saying "please," "thank you," "excuse me," or addressing people by their proper titles—can go a long way toward positive communication.

Politeness does not mean hiding who they are. It just means adding respectful touches to their natural style. If a Sagittarius is unsure, they can watch how others behave in that setting and adapt. Over time, it becomes easier to switch between casual chats and polite talk, depending on the situation.

Communicating in Groups vs. One-on-One

Sagittarians might find that their style differs when speaking to a group versus having a personal conversation. In a group, they can bring energy, share ideas, and encourage interaction. They might be good at making sure the discussion does not stall. However, they should also be careful not to dominate, letting quieter members have a turn.

In one-on-one chats, Sagittarians can be more focused and personal. They can show empathy, nod along, and dive deeper into a friend's or coworker's thoughts. One-on-one talks allow them to truly listen and connect. It is good for Sagittarians to understand these differences so they can adjust the pace and tone to fit each situation.

Digital Communication and Social Media

Many people today communicate a lot through social media and digital platforms. Sagittarians often enjoy these tools because they can connect with different folks, share articles or fun facts, and post about their interests. They might have various friends online, from different backgrounds, which suits their love of variety. But digital communication has a few pitfalls:

- **Tone Misunderstandings:** Text-only chats do not always show tone. A friendly tease might seem harsh if there is no face or voice attached.

- **Overcommitment:** A Sagittarius might join lots of online groups or chat threads, but struggle to keep up. It can be helpful to limit the number of online groups to a few that matter the most.

- **Privacy Concerns:** Oversharing personal details, photos, or strong opinions can cause issues. Taking a moment to think, "Am I comfortable with anyone reading this?" helps them post responsibly.

By managing their online presence wisely, Sagittarians can enjoy the benefits of digital communication without risking misunderstandings or burnout.

Speaking With Empathy

When giving advice or feedback, Sagittarians can remember to speak from a place of empathy. Instead of only stating their view, they can include a phrase like, "I hear what you're saying," or "I understand why you might feel that way." This shows the other person that their feelings have been acknowledged. It does not mean the Sagittarius must agree with everything the other person says. Rather, it is about showing understanding and respect.

Empathy also means picking up on hints about someone's mood. If the other person seems sad or stressed, a direct or harsh comment might make them feel worse. Sagittarians can use their natural sensitivity to sense this and adjust. For example, if a friend is clearly upset, a calmer, caring tone is likely better than a joking or rushed style.

Collaborative Communication

In group projects or team tasks, a Sagittarius can excel when they realize that communication is a team effort. They do not have to come up with every idea alone, nor do they always need to lead. Instead, they can encourage everyone to pitch in. This might mean asking quieter group members, "What do you think?" or "Do you have any ideas?" By pulling others into the discussion, they create a sense of unity.

Also, if a Sagittarius disagrees with a team decision, they can learn to express that disagreement constructively. Rather than shutting the idea down, they might say, "I'm concerned about this part. Maybe we can make a small change." This approach keeps the spirit of collaboration alive, even when conflicts arise.

Cultural Sensitivity

Sagittarians often enjoy learning about different traditions and perspectives, which can help them in cross-cultural communication. Still, they must remember that not every culture uses the same gestures, humor, or directness. What seems normal to a Sagittarius might be strange or even rude in another cultural context.

Taking a moment to learn basic customs—like whether eye contact is polite, how close you can stand, or if certain hand gestures are offensive—can make a big difference. Sagittarians who respect these differences show genuine regard for the people they talk to. It also helps avoid confusion that might come from mismatched communication styles.

Handling Criticism or Negative Feedback

When a Sagittarius hears negative feedback, they might feel defensive or think the other person is being unfair. But part of good communication is absorbing feedback without letting emotions take over. Instead of firing back with reasons why they are right, Sagittarians can practice saying, "Thank you for letting me know. I'll think about that."

Later, they can decide if the feedback was valid and how to act on it. Not every piece of feedback is correct, but staying calm keeps the conversation respectful. If they do believe the other person is wrong, they can state their side in a polite manner, like, "I see where you're coming from. However, here's my perspective." Maintaining composure helps them keep their credibility.

Teaching and Explaining

Sagittarians are often eager to pass along what they know. Whether helping a friend with a new hobby or guiding a coworker in a task, they enjoy sharing information in a relaxed, encouraging tone. Still, teaching effectively means breaking things down into steps and checking if the other person is following. A Sagittarius who rushes through an explanation might leave the learner confused.

Asking small questions like, "Does that make sense?" or "Want me to show that again?" can create a friendly feedback loop. If the other person is lost, they can say so before more confusion builds up. This method fosters a comfortable environment where the learner feels safe to ask questions, and the Sagittarius can adjust the pace as needed.

Sharing Stories

Sagittarians sometimes love telling stories about their experiences or interesting events they have heard about. These stories can be a great way to connect with people, especially if they involve humor or eye-opening details. However, it helps to keep the story focused and not wander off topic for too long. People might get impatient if the story has too many side details.

A helpful tip is to watch the listener's reactions. If they seem eager and engaged, the Sagittarius can keep going. If they look confused or are glancing away, it might be time to wrap up. A short line like, "Anyway, that's what happened, and I thought it was neat," can provide a natural closing. Ending at the right time leaves a positive impression.

Confidence With Sensitivity

Sagittarians tend to exude a certain boldness. This can give them an advantage when speaking in front of groups or meeting new people. However, they should also remember that not everyone is drawn to that bold style right away. A shy person might need a gentler approach. Leading a conversation with a quieter tone or a friendly question can make the shy person feel more comfortable than an energetic blast of chatter.

Being sensitive to others' personalities helps a Sagittarius avoid accidentally overwhelming them. Over time, the two can reach a middle ground where the quieter person feels safe expressing themselves, and the Sagittarius can still be their upbeat self.

Conflict vs. Discussion

A common communication issue is the difference between healthy discussion and conflict that becomes personal. If a Sagittarius is discussing a strong opinion, it can shift into conflict if frustration builds up. They might raise their voice or use words that sound like personal attacks. To keep it from going that far, they can remind themselves, "We're discussing an idea, not the person."

Phrases like, "I disagree with that point" are more respectful than, "You're wrong," because they separate the idea from the individual. By focusing on the topic, a Sagittarius can keep the door open for ongoing dialogue. If things heat up, they can suggest a short pause—maybe stepping away for a moment—then returning to the discussion once both sides have cooled down.

Maintaining Interest in Others

Sometimes, Sagittarians get wrapped up in their own exciting ideas and forget to ask about the other person's news or experiences. A balanced communication style includes genuine interest in what others have to share. A simple question like, "How has your day been?" or "What's going on in your life?" can show real curiosity.

Following up with thoughtful comments—like, "That sounds tough," or "Wow, that's really fun"—encourages the other person to open up more. By giving space for others to speak, a Sagittarius creates mutual understanding instead of a one-sided conversation. This habit also helps them learn fresh perspectives they might have missed if they only focused on themselves.

CHAPTER 10: LIKES & DISLIKES

Sagittarius individuals often have clear preferences about many things in life, from hobbies and activities to personal values and everyday routines. Because they value variety, these preferences can range widely and can change if they find something new that sparks their interest. In this chapter, we will look at specific things Sagittarians often enjoy and those they tend to avoid. This will give more understanding of their tastes without repeating the same points covered in earlier chapters.

Love of Exploration

One of the major things many Sagittarians like is the chance to explore. This can mean different things. For some, it might involve trying food from other places or learning about distant cultures. For others, it might be reading about new scientific developments or investigating new hobbies. The key idea is that they are curious and open. They want to see, hear, or taste something they have never experienced before.

This love of exploration can make them eager to visit new neighborhoods, check out local events, or watch documentaries that spark fresh thoughts. They might have a list of places they want to visit someday or topics they want to learn more about. If their world starts to feel too familiar, they may look for new ways to satisfy this craving for discovery.

Enjoyment of Physical Activities

Many Sagittarians appreciate physical activities that let them use their energy. This could be playing sports, going on a brisk walk, or dancing around at home. Some of them might sign up for group sports teams, while others prefer solo forms of exercise, like running or yoga-like stretches. They often enjoy the way movement and exercise helps them feel alive and keeps boredom at bay.

They do not need to be extreme athletes to like movement. Even smaller acts—like riding a bike around the block or tossing a ball with friends—can bring them joy. The important part is that it lets them shake off restlessness. If they cannot find ways to move around, they might start feeling caged in and unhappy.

A Strong Pull Toward Learning

Sagittarius individuals usually love learning new facts or skills. They might watch videos about outer space, historical events, or how to do a craft. Their natural curiosity leads them to pick up random pieces of knowledge and store them away for future conversations. If they find a topic truly fascinating, they may spend hours reading about it, even if it is not related to their job or school work.

This enjoyment of learning also shows up in group chats. A Sagittarius might say, "I just found out this amazing fact!" then launch into an explanation. Their friends might appreciate the fresh knowledge, or at least get a laugh out of how excited they are. If a Sagittarius feels stuck in an environment that does not offer new information, they can grow bored and restless.

Socializing With Friends

Sagittarians often enjoy spending time with friends, especially when the setting allows for laughter and animated talk. They might invite people over for casual game nights, fun group tasks, or simple cookouts. They also tend to be open to last-minute plans, like going to a movie in the evening if they learn about a good showtime that day.

Still, they are not always the ones who want huge, loud parties. Some Sagittarians prefer smaller gatherings where they can actually talk and share stories. The main point is that they like being around positive, open-minded folks who are up for conversation or silly jokes. If a social event feels too formal, they might find it dull and look for a corner to chat more freely.

Having Personal Space

Even though Sagittarians enjoy being around people, they also want their own personal space at times. They do not like feeling monitored or bossed around. If someone tries to set too many rules on them—like where they can go or how they can spend their time—they may become annoyed. They might need a spot at home that is purely theirs, or time in the day to do what they feel like doing.

They also appreciate flexible schedules. If a plan is set in stone for weeks, a Sagittarius might feel locked in. They want to know there is some room to do something else if they get a new idea. A day that is too fully booked can leave them feeling tired before it even starts. Having at least a small window for spontaneous actions can boost their mood.

Favorite Types of Hobbies

While every Sagittarius is unique, there are some hobbies that many of them tend to enjoy:

1. **Outdoor Activities:** Hiking, strolling through a park, or visiting outdoor fairs can be appealing.

2. **Creative Projects:** Drawing, painting, or crafting can be a fun way to express ideas.

3. **Reading and Research:** They might like exploring topics from science to fantasy, often picking up books or articles that expand their knowledge.

4. **Sports or Fitness:** Anything that keeps them moving can be attractive, from simple workouts to casual sports.

5. **Music or Performing:** Some Sagittarians enjoy playing instruments or singing, especially if it helps them share a bright spirit.

Again, not every Sagittarius will match these exactly, but these areas often pop up as points of interest.

Liking Cheerful Surroundings

Sagittarius people often like surroundings that feel bright and positive. They might add colorful decorations to their room or choose clothing with bold patterns. If they have an office or a desk, they might place fun items or photos around to keep the space from feeling bland. Even if their style is simple, they usually enjoy some kind of personal touch in their environment.

They can also enjoy background music or other cheerful elements in a space. Silence might feel heavy if they want to keep their energy level up. A bit of lively music, a friendly chatter, or even a bright wall color can make them feel more at home. When a room feels too dull or closed in, they might feel restless or uninspired.

Appreciation of Humor

Sagittarians generally love a good laugh, whether it is watching a funny movie, trading jokes, or telling silly stories among friends. They often use humor as a way to connect and relax. A good comedic show or a clever cartoon might be on their list of favorites. Joking around with others can be a highlight of their day, as long as the jokes stay lighthearted and not hurtful.

They also tend to be drawn to people who can joke back and keep the comedic flow going. An environment that is too serious or tense all the time might make them uncomfortable. Of course, they know certain moments require respect. But having space for laughter is a key part of what they like in daily life.

Dislike of Boredom and Routine

One major dislike for many Sagittarians is boredom. They do not enjoy being stuck doing the same thing for hours or days without a change. Repetitive chores or tasks can feel like a trap, draining their energy. For instance, if they have to do a very mechanical job—like entering the same data over and over—they might feel restless.

They also tend to dislike too much routine. Doing the same steps every day at exactly the same time can make them want to break free. Sometimes, they will try to add small twists, like taking a new route to work or adding a quick creative task during a break. This helps them fight off that sense of dull repetition.

Distaste for Dishonesty

Sagittarians often value honesty, so they have a strong dislike for dishonesty. Whether it is lying, cheating, or hiding big facts, they usually find it hard to respect someone who is not straightforward. If they catch someone being fake or manipulative, they might confront them or decide to spend less time around them. They want clarity, even if the truth is not always pleasant.

They can also get upset if they feel forced to act in a dishonest way. For example, if a friend suggests a scheme to trick another person, a Sagittarius might refuse or feel uneasy. They want to stay true to themselves and not get tangled in lies. This can mean they are better off in groups that also respect honesty.

Dislike of Close-Minded Behavior

Because Sagittarians love new thoughts and openness, they often dislike close-minded attitudes. If someone refuses to consider any viewpoint other than their own, the Sagittarius might feel frustrated. They may try to nudge the person toward open-mindedness. If that does not work, they might distance themselves rather than argue.

This does not mean they expect everyone to agree with them. Instead, they simply appreciate the willingness to listen and think about different angles. If people shut down conversations or use harsh criticism without real thought, it clashes with the Sagittarius view that there is always more to learn.

Mixed Feelings About Details

Sagittarians can dislike tasks that revolve around tiny details. They would often rather jump into the bigger concept than get stuck reading every line of fine print. When a process demands close attention to each small piece, they might drag their feet or find ways to speed it up. They can see these details as blocks preventing them from exploring bigger ideas.

Still, some Sagittarians learn to push past this dislike by looking at the final goal. If the detail work is necessary to achieve a result they care about, they might power through. However, if the detail work feels pointless or never-ending, they can grow irritated. Having a friend or partner who enjoys detail-oriented tasks can be a great help for them.

Enjoying Friendly Debates

Strangely enough, Sagittarians often like friendly debates. They do not mind discussing strong opinions or diving into big subjects, like moral issues or current events, as long as the debate stays respectful. They find it stimulating to swap viewpoints. A lively back-and-forth can keep them engaged, and they might even shift their stance if the other side presents a convincing argument.

However, they do not like debates that turn mean or personal. If the other person starts making attacks instead of discussing ideas, a Sagittarius might either get upset or exit the discussion. They want a debate where everyone keeps a decent tone and focuses on facts or logical points, not insults.

Love for Spontaneous Outings

Sagittarians may enjoy random outings that break the routine. For example, if a friend says, "Let's go on a small road trip tomorrow," they might jump at the chance—provided they do not have firm responsibilities that block it. They like these spur-of-the-moment decisions because it feeds their sense of adventure. It also fits with their preference for freedom, letting them do something fresh without too much prior planning.

Of course, not every Sagittarius is equally spontaneous. Some may prefer to plan a bit. But in general, they appreciate having the option to shift plans if a cool idea pops up. They do not enjoy environments where every minute of the day is rigidly planned out weeks in advance.

Tastes in Entertainment

When it comes to entertainment, a Sagittarius might lean toward things that either make them laugh or teach them something. Comedies, documentaries, travel shows, or interesting stories about real-life events often catch their attention. They may also enjoy dramatic shows with big ideas or explorations of different cultures. If it sparks their mind or humor, they are in.

They may avoid forms of entertainment that they see as too slow or negative, unless there is a clever twist. For instance, a very sad movie without a hopeful message might not appeal to them. They prefer something that leaves them either feeling uplifted or at least more informed about the world.

Favorite Places

Sagittarians often enjoy places that have some element of openness or possibility. This can include:

- **Nature Spots:** Beaches, parks, or mountains, where they can move around and see wide views.

- **Lively Cafés or Bookstores:** Spots that encourage discussion or new ideas. A cozy bookstore with interesting books can be a real treat.

- **Cultural Centers:** Museums or places showcasing art, science, or history. They like seeing new exhibits or learning tidbits they did not know before.

- **Casual Social Hubs:** Informal restaurants or hangouts where friends can chat freely and maybe watch a game or listen to music.

They might feel restless in cramped or overly formal settings for too long. If they have to be in a fancy place that requires strict manners, they can manage, but it will not be their preferred spot to relax.

Dislike of Unnecessary Drama

While Sagittarians can handle spirited debates, they usually dislike personal drama that goes in circles. If a friend group is constantly fighting over small misunderstandings, a Sagittarius might step away or try to fix it quickly. They prefer a sense of harmony and forward thinking, rather than rehashing old grudges again and again.

They also dislike it when people twist facts or stir up rumors just to cause tension. Because Sagittarians value honesty and directness, manipulative behavior gets on their nerves. They might end up confronting the source of the drama or politely removing themselves from the group if it persists.

Attraction to Wide Horizons

The symbol of Sagittarius is often linked with aiming for something far away. This aligns with their enjoyment of anything that suggests a broader horizon. They might like open fields, a chance to look at city lights from a tall building, or gazing at the sky filled with stars. These sights stir their imagination and remind them of the bigger world outside everyday details.

This preference can also apply in a figurative sense, like thinking about "the bigger picture" in life rather than focusing on small concerns. They might spend time daydreaming about the future or about things they wish to learn. It ties back to their general love of possibilities and dislike for limits that feel too narrow.

Foods and Culinary Adventures

Although tastes vary, many Sagittarians enjoy trying foods from different cuisines. They might be open to spicy dishes, unusual flavors, or interesting cooking styles they have never encountered before. Going to a restaurant that offers "something different" can be an exciting event for them. They may also like the social aspect of sharing dishes with friends.

However, if they are forced to eat the same plain meal day after day, they will likely get fed up. Switching up their diet or adding small variations can keep them happier. Some Sagittarians might experiment with cooking at home, mixing ingredients in creative ways that surprise their family or roommates.

Dislike of Restrictive Rules

We have touched on this earlier in different contexts, but it is worth stating clearly: Sagittarians often have a strong dislike for restrictions that feel unnecessary. Rules that stifle personal choice or block harmless forms of self-expression can irritate them. For example, if a workplace or school enforces a dress code that is overly strict, a Sagittarius might feel annoyed and want to find small ways to personalize their look.

However, they can accept rules that make sense for safety or fairness. The difference is that they want a clear reason behind them. If a rule seems random or purely controlling, it clashes with their sense of freedom. They might challenge or question such a rule, hoping to see it changed.

Interest in Personal Growth

Despite their dislike of repetition, Sagittarians tend to enjoy activities that help them become better at something. This might be practicing an instrument, learning a language, or developing a new skill they find cool. They like challenges, especially if each step feels like progress. They might learn a martial art or a dance style, as it blends movement with personal improvement.

While they do not always stick to the same routine, they might keep coming back to something that truly interests them, even if they take breaks in between. They like seeing how they have advanced over time, which reaffirms their sense that life is full of interesting paths.

Preferences for Personal Style

In terms of personal style or appearance, Sagittarians often prefer clothes or accessories that feel comfortable yet expressive. They might choose bright colors, quirky patterns, or items that remind them of places they have visited. Some might wear casual outfits most of the time, since they do not like feeling constrained by stiff clothing.

They also might enjoy collecting little keepsakes from experiences—a keychain from a memorable trip, a bracelet that holds personal meaning, or a shirt with a unique design. These items help them recall the variety and openness they love, turning their wardrobe or living space into a reflection of their adventures and interests.

Mood Music and Fun Sounds

Music can play a big role in a Sagittarius's day. They might have playlists for different moods—energetic songs to start the morning, chill tunes to wind down, or uplifting tracks to keep them motivated while they work or do chores. They can enjoy a wide range of genres, from pop and rock to global beats or indie music, as long as it sparks a certain feeling.

They might also link certain songs to good memories, like a special event or a trip with friends. Playing that tune again can instantly bring them back to that happy moment. If they feel down, turning on a favorite song can help shift their emotions to a lighter place.

Balance Between Likes and Dislikes

While Sagittarians have clear likes (freedom, variety, open-mindedness) and dislikes (boredom, dishonesty, too many rigid rules), it is important they learn to handle both sides in a balanced way. For example, they cannot always escape routine tasks, so they may try to insert bits of creativity into those tasks. They also cannot avoid every rule, so they might look for ways to make peace with the rules that do exist.

By staying aware of what energizes them and what drags them down, they can shape their environment to be more comfortable. This might mean picking a job that allows them to move around or focusing on friends who share their sense of curiosity. It might also mean politely pushing for change when they face rules that seem unfair, but doing so with respect and reason.

CHAPTER 11: SAGITTARIUS & OTHER ZODIAC SIGNS

Sagittarius people often bring an upbeat, free-spirited vibe to relationships. Whether it is friendship, family ties, or working side by side, they usually carry a spark of positivity and open-mindedness. At the same time, each zodiac sign has its own style and priorities. When Sagittarius interacts with the other signs, some connections might feel as smooth as a warm breeze, while others may require patience or compromise. In this chapter, we will look at how Sagittarius tends to get along with each zodiac sign, focusing on what they can learn from each other and which points might need extra care. We will not repeat the guidance from earlier chapters, but instead share fresh observations about these pairings.

General Thoughts on Zodiac Compatibility

When people talk about the zodiac, they sometimes ask, "Which signs get along best?" There is no single answer, because every person is unique. Still, looking at basic traits can offer clues about what might work smoothly or cause friction. Sagittarius is linked with a need for freedom, honesty, and positivity. Signs that accept or match these traits may connect well, while signs that crave structure or privacy might clash at times.

At the same time, differences do not always cause problems. Sometimes, these differences allow both sides to learn. A practical, detail-focused sign might help Sagittarius become more organized, and Sagittarius might help a more cautious sign take bold steps. Let's look at each sign and see how it pairs with Sagittarius.

Sagittarius and Aries

Similarity in Fire Energy
Aries is another Fire sign. Both Sagittarius and Aries tend to be lively, direct, and full of energy. They can spark each other's enthusiasm, enjoying activities and adventures. If they are friends, they might try sports or playful competitions. In work settings, their combined passion can lead to new ideas.

Potential for Impulsive Decisions
Both Aries and Sagittarius may jump into plans without detailed thinking. This can be exciting, but if they take on big challenges together, they might overlook practical steps. Learning to slow down at times can help them avoid mishaps. Still, the bond often remains strong because they understand each other's love of action.

Handling Disagreements
When two Fire signs argue, sparks can fly. However, Aries and Sagittarius usually say what they think, get it out in the open, and then move on. They often do not hold grudges for long. As long as each respects the other's viewpoint, arguments can end fairly quickly.

Sagittarius and Taurus

Differences in Approach
Taurus is an Earth sign that values stability and comfort. Sagittarius prefers variety and might feel unsettled if they get stuck in one place. Taurus may wonder why Sagittarius seems restless, and Sagittarius might feel Taurus is too fixed in routines.

Finding Common Ground
They can learn from each other if they stay open-minded. Taurus can show Sagittarius how to appreciate everyday comforts and the importance of finishing tasks before rushing off. Meanwhile,

Sagittarius might help Taurus see the fun in trying something new once in a while.

Dealing With Pace
Taurus often moves at a slower speed, thinking carefully before making changes. Sagittarius, on the other hand, might make swift choices. This can frustrate both sides unless they find a middle ground. Sagittarius can practice patience, and Taurus can allow a bit of spontaneity.

Sagittarius and Gemini

Shared Love of Information
Gemini is an Air sign known for curiosity and quick thinking. Sagittarius also loves to learn new things, though from a broader perspective. Together, they can have lively talks that jump from one topic to another. They can make great companions if they want to discover interesting facts, share stories, or plan small outings.

Possible Issue: Restlessness
Both Gemini and Sagittarius might jump from idea to idea. If they need to finish a group project, staying focused can be a challenge. They may need some structure or reminders to stay on track, especially if a deadline is close.

Social Connection
These two signs often enjoy meeting people and exploring fresh environments. They might go to events, workshops, or clubs together. Their combined curiosity can make them the life of the party, though they should also remember to let each other express personal opinions fully, without interruption.

Sagittarius and Cancer

Difference in Emotional Style
Cancer is a Water sign that tends to focus on feelings, home life, and nurturing bonds. Sagittarius focuses on possibilities, new experiences, and honesty. Cancer might think Sagittarius is too blunt or distant from deeper emotions. Meanwhile, Sagittarius could feel Cancer worries too much or stays stuck in past issues.

Balancing Openness and Sensitivity
If they respect each other's needs, these two can form a caring bond. Cancer can show Sagittarius how to connect with emotional depth, while Sagittarius can help Cancer adopt a more optimistic outlook. The main key is gentle communication. Sagittarius should avoid being too frank when Cancer is feeling sensitive.

Shared Growth
Cancer might help Sagittarius appreciate the comfort of a stable home base, and Sagittarius can encourage Cancer to step out of their comfort zone occasionally. They have to accept that they move at different speeds when it comes to change, so patience is crucial.

Sagittarius and Leo

A Bright Fire Pairing
Leo, another Fire sign, often shares Sagittarius's sunny outlook. Both signs like to have fun, be creative, and express themselves openly. They can light up a room with laughter and stories, making them a lively duo in social groups.

Wanting Attention
Leo sometimes desires the spotlight, while Sagittarius also likes to share big ideas. If both want center stage at the same time, it might lead to minor clashes. However, if they take turns letting the other shine, they can form a supportive pair.

Cheering Each Other On
Because both are positive, they can motivate one another. When one has a bright plan, the other often joins in with excitement. Challenges can be tackled by blending Leo's self-confidence with Sagittarius's sense of adventure. Together, they can accomplish impressive feats, as long as they stay mindful of each other's pride and perspective.

Sagittarius and Virgo

Clash of Big Ideas and Details
Virgo is an Earth sign that is practical, detail-focused, and likes order. Sagittarius often looks at the big picture, sometimes skipping small steps. Virgo may see Sagittarius as disorganized or too quick. Sagittarius might see Virgo as too fussy or careful.

Learning From Each Other
In a positive scenario, Virgo can help Sagittarius slow down, plan thoroughly, and see the importance of details. Meanwhile, Sagittarius can help Virgo relax, take breaks, and discover a world beyond lists and routines. They can develop respect by acknowledging the value each side brings.

Clear Communication
Because Virgo pays close attention to words and meaning, while Sagittarius can speak frankly, they should be sure to phrase feedback kindly. Virgo might notice mistakes in what Sagittarius says, and Sagittarius should not take that as criticism of their entire character. With fair communication, they can avoid resentment.

Sagittarius and Libra

Shared Sociable Nature
Libra, an Air sign, likes harmony and partnerships. Sagittarius, with its friendly disposition, can match well with Libra in social settings.

They can have thoughtful talks about fairness, justice, or creative topics. Libra's sense of balance might calm Sagittarius's occasional rush.

Risk of Indecision
Libra sometimes struggles to decide, wanting to keep everyone happy. Sagittarius might get impatient, wanting to move forward without too much debate. If they collaborate, Libra can weigh options carefully, and Sagittarius can provide the spark to make a final choice.

Enjoying Life's Pleasures
Both can enjoy cultural events, pleasant atmospheres, and gatherings with interesting people. They might love going to places like art galleries or nice restaurants, where they can chat, explore, and share impressions. The main issue is finding a pace that suits them both—Libra might move more slowly than Sagittarius, but with open discussion, they can adapt.

Sagittarius and Scorpio

Powerful Energy
Scorpio is a Water sign, often intense and private. Sagittarius is open and straightforward. Scorpio might find Sagittarius too open with personal matters, while Sagittarius might think Scorpio is keeping secrets. This can create friction unless they both try to understand each other's boundaries.

Diving Deep vs. Exploring Wide
Scorpio likes to dig into deep issues, studying them thoroughly. Sagittarius likes to roam across broad subjects, picking up bits of knowledge. If they work together, Scorpio can encourage Sagittarius to look deeper, and Sagittarius can show Scorpio the joy of exploring many areas without getting stuck in one.

Trust and Honesty
Scorpio values loyalty and sincerity. Sagittarius, being honest, can build trust if they handle Scorpio's emotions carefully. At times, Sagittarius might not sense how deeply Scorpio feels, so they should avoid making jokes about serious topics that matter to Scorpio. Good communication can help them find mutual respect.

Sagittarius and Sagittarius

Similar Outlook
When two Sagittarians team up, they can share a life full of enthusiasm, big ideas, and humor. They often understand each other's need for freedom, so they are less likely to feel controlled. They may enjoy traveling, starting projects, or swapping interesting information.

Potential Problems
If both avoid routine tasks, their shared living space or plans can get messy. They might forget responsibilities if they are too busy having fun. Also, blunt remarks might sting if neither invests enough care into how they speak. But because they share the same sign, they can learn from each other's mistakes and strengths.

Supporting Growth
Two Sagittarians can spark growth by pushing each other to try fresh experiences. However, they should stay mindful of practical matters—paying bills, finishing tasks, and so on. If they develop a plan for handling everyday duties, they can keep their free spirit alive without chaos.

Sagittarius and Capricorn

Different Approaches to Goals
Capricorn is an Earth sign focused on long-term goals, structure, and steady progress. Sagittarius is more free-flowing, preferring

flexibility over strict planning. Capricorn might see Sagittarius as scattered, while Sagittarius might see Capricorn as too rigid.

Learning Balance

If they work together, Capricorn can provide a solid foundation and help Sagittarius create a plan for bigger dreams. Meanwhile, Sagittarius can remind Capricorn to relax and appreciate the smaller joys of life. They may clash if Capricorn presses too hard on rules or if Sagittarius refuses to follow any structure at all. Clear boundaries help.

Steady Progress vs. Quick Moves

Capricorn moves methodically, wanting stability. Sagittarius can bring creative solutions that speed up progress. They can form a good team if they talk openly about timelines and methods. Each sign gains from the other's viewpoint: Capricorn learns to be more open to changes, and Sagittarius discovers the power of steady effort.

Sagittarius and Aquarius

Shared Love of Ideas

Aquarius, an Air sign, loves thinking outside the box and discussing big concepts. Sagittarius also enjoys big thoughts and a wide perspective. Their talks can be thrilling, jumping from scientific topics to social issues to possible inventions. Both signs value independence, so they usually respect each other's space.

Possible Emotional Distance

Neither Aquarius nor Sagittarius is known for heavy emotional displays. They might have trouble offering deep comfort if one of them feels sad. Learning to slow down and address feelings can help them support each other better. However, because both prefer logical chats, they often feel quite comfortable together.

Encouraging Each Other's Freedom

Aquarius stands for freedom and uniqueness, while Sagittarius loves open possibilities. They can inspire each other to follow new paths or research interesting subjects. As friends or colleagues, they might form a group that runs exciting community projects or shares knowledge. The main caution is to remember empathy in case someone does need emotional care.

Sagittarius and Pisces

Blend of Fire and Water

Pisces is a Water sign known for empathy, imagination, and sensitivity. Sagittarius is more direct, bright, and flexible. Pisces might be drawn to Sagittarius's positivity, while Sagittarius may find Pisces's dreamy nature intriguing. Yet they can have misunderstandings if Sagittarius speaks too bluntly or dismisses Pisces's feelings.

Balancing Reality and Dreams

Pisces sometimes drifts into daydreams. Sagittarius, with its hopeful viewpoint, can encourage Pisces to think about possibilities. But Sagittarius also likes a certain level of realism when making decisions, even if they do not dwell on details. They may need to check if their goals line up. Pisces might want a more emotional environment, while Sagittarius wants more open activity.

Communication With Care

Since Pisces feels emotions strongly, Sagittarius should be mindful not to speak in an offhand manner about topics that Pisces cares about. Pisces, on the other hand, can learn to be more open about expressing needs instead of assuming Sagittarius will guess. Honest, gentle talks can help them grow closer.

Tips for Sagittarius Interacting With Each Sign

While each Sagittarius is different, here are some brief tips for dealing with potential ups and downs across the zodiac:

Aries: Encourage each other to think before acting. Plan some details, even if briefly.

Taurus: Show patience. Try to see the value in slow and steady moves. Give Taurus some excitement without scaring them off.

Gemini: Set small goals together so both of you finish what you start. Enjoy curious discussions, but remember time limits.

Cancer: Respect emotions. Talk openly, but gently. Find shared comfort in positive thinking and a warm home setting.

Leo: Share the spotlight. Praise each other's achievements. Use your combined confidence for group benefit.

Virgo: Mix Virgo's methodical approach with your enthusiasm. Listen carefully to advice about details.

Libra: Help them decide faster, but also let them weigh options. Enjoy social events together.

Scorpio: Keep trust strong. Respect Scorpio's deeper feelings. Encourage them to talk, but do not push too hard.

Sagittarius: Avoid double chaos. Divide chores or tasks clearly so you both can stay on track.

Capricorn: Combine your energy with their structure. Show them how to lighten up, and let them guide you on stable planning.

Aquarius: Embrace shared independence. Enjoy exploring new concepts. Just remember to address emotional needs if they arise.

Pisces: Practice gentle honesty. Listen to their creative ideas. Encourage open communication so feelings are not hidden.

Looking Beyond Sun Signs

In astrology, people also talk about Moon signs, rising signs, and other placements. These factors can shift how strongly someone displays their "main" zodiac traits. For instance, a person with a Sagittarius Sun but a Virgo Moon could be more detail-oriented than the usual Sagittarius. Meanwhile, a Taurus Sun with a Sagittarius rising might seem a bit more spontaneous than a typical Taurus.

All these layers mean actual compatibility is more complex than just matching Sun signs. Still, the points above can offer a broad sense of how Sagittarius might relate to others. When meeting new people, Sagittarians can stay open to surprises, because one person's chart might have a blend of traits that fit very well with Sagittarius energy.

Positive Outcomes of Zodiac Differences

While some differences in zodiac traits can lead to misunderstandings, they can also lead to growth. For Sagittarius, working with or befriending people who think differently can provide new insights. A sign that loves organization might help Sagittarius keep track of tasks, while Sagittarius can show that same sign the fun side of being spontaneous. Learning from each other can create a balanced environment where strengths are shared and weaknesses are softened.

For example, a Sagittarius and a Virgo might start off seeing each other as mismatched—one is messy, the other is neat. But if they recognize the good side of each trait, they can team up effectively. Virgo might handle detailed plans, while Sagittarius secures bright opportunities and new connections. This mix can lead to successful projects, fun friendship dynamics, or even strong family bonds.

Ways Sagittarius Can Thrive in Mixed-Groups

In big groups with many different signs, Sagittarius can often act as a unifying force. They are usually friendly, open to varied viewpoints, and not quick to judge. Here are a few ways they can do well:

Suggest Group Activities: Because Sagittarians like variety, they might propose interesting events that appeal to multiple personalities. This could help bring the group together.

Encourage Free Discussion: When others hold back, Sagittarius can ask questions to draw them out. Their direct style can help break the ice.

Stay Respectful: With signs that are more private or sensitive, a gentle approach can ensure nobody feels pushed. Sagittarius can balance their lively energy with genuine listening.

Offer Optimism: When tensions rise, a Sagittarius's hopeful viewpoint can calm nerves. They might remind everyone of the group's shared goals or good moments from the past.

Avoiding Common Sagittarius Pitfalls in Relationships

Though Sagittarius has many strong qualities, a few pitfalls can appear when relating to other signs:

Being Too Blunt: Honesty is good, but if it is delivered harshly, it might cause hurt. Softer wording helps.

Skipping Details: Some signs need thorough planning. Sagittarius can show respect by at least considering important facts.

Restless Commitment: If they give their word but lose interest, that can upset more steady signs. They should keep promises or communicate if plans must change.

Avoiding Emotional Depth: Some signs need emotional closeness. Sagittarius can learn to sit with heavy feelings when required, rather than making a quick joke.

Embracing Shared Adventures With Other Signs

One of the best parts about being a Sagittarius is the ability to bring fun and a sense of possibility to various relationships. They often inspire friends and family to try experiences they might not have considered. Here are ways that can play out with different signs:

Adventures With Aries or Leo: Enjoy active outings, creative tasks, or friendly competitions.

Curious Chats With Gemini or Aquarius: Research interesting topics, attend local talks, or try new technology.

Grounded Activity With Taurus, Virgo, or Capricorn: Blend learning with practical tasks, like cooking or gardening, to keep them engaged.

Emotional Sharing With Cancer, Scorpio, or Pisces: Balance the desire for novelty with gentler moments. Maybe watch a touching movie or visit a calm nature spot.

Sharing Lighthearted Energy With Libra: Plan social gatherings where everyone can mingle and share ideas.

By adjusting the type of activity to match the other person's comfort zone, Sagittarius can strengthen bonds without forcing others too far from what they enjoy.

Working and Collaborating Across the Zodiac

In a professional or academic environment, Sagittarius can shine by:

Respecting Each Sign's Strengths: Let the detail-loving signs handle detailed tasks, and let the big-picture thinkers co-create overall plans.

Staying Flexible: If a coworker or classmate has a different method, a Sagittarius can adapt while still injecting positivity.

Being Inclusive: They can ensure everyone's ideas are heard, bridging differences in approach or pace.

Showing Patience: Not everyone moves as fast as Sagittarius. Giving others time to share or think is a sign of respect.

Family Ties Among Different Signs

In a family where each member is a different zodiac sign, interactions can be quite varied. A Sagittarius child might ask for room to explore interests, while a more cautious sign might want firm boundaries. Open talks about each person's needs can reduce tension. For instance:

Parents or Siblings Who Are Earth Signs (Taurus, Virgo, Capricorn): They might emphasize chores, schedules, or caution. The Sagittarius child can still thrive if given breaks for free play or reading.

Family Members Who Are Water Signs (Cancer, Scorpio, Pisces): They might be more emotional. The Sagittarius teen can learn to offer comfort by listening closely before offering jokes or solutions.

Fire Sign Relatives (Aries, Leo): Lots of high energy. Watch out for noisy disagreements, but also enjoy shared adventures.

Air Sign Relatives (Gemini, Libra, Aquarius): Talkative household. Be sure to switch topics sometimes so no one feels overwhelmed.

Friendships That Cross Zodiac Boundaries

Friendships often form across all kinds of signs. For Sagittarius, the key is to appreciate the uniqueness of each friend. Some might be the perfect partner for trying fresh sports or traveling somewhere new. Others might be better for calm nights at home or deep emotional talks. By respecting each friend's natural style, a Sagittarius can keep a wide circle of meaningful connections. They do not have to force every friend into the same mold, and the variety often keeps life interesting.

Navigating Love Connections

Relationships that go beyond friendship can bring deeper challenges and joys. The sign of the romantic partner might heavily influence what they expect from love, closeness, or future plans. A few notes:

If the Partner Is an Earth Sign: They might crave long-term security, so the Sagittarius can show they can be reliable when it counts.

If the Partner Is a Fire Sign: Both might be energetic, but arguments should be handled carefully so they do not flare up.

If the Partner Is an Air Sign: Expect lively conversations and mutual respect for freedom, which fits well. But watch out for ignoring emotional issues.

If the Partner Is a Water Sign: Build trust by listening and offering genuine care, not just short optimism.

CHAPTER 12: SAGITTARIUS THROUGH THE AGES

Sagittarius traits can show themselves in different ways depending on a person's age and life stage. A Sagittarius child might display bright curiosity at home, while a teenager might be bursting with new ideas at school. As they grow into adulthood, these qualities often mature, leading to changes in how Sagittarians relate to their family, friends, and the wider world. In this chapter, we will look at how Sagittarius characteristics emerge at various phases—from childhood through later years—without repeating details covered in previous chapters. We will add fresh insights on challenges and opportunities a Sagittarius may face at each stage.

Early Childhood (Roughly Ages 1–5)

Natural Curiosity in Toddlers
Even small Sagittarius children can show curiosity early on. They might crawl or walk around looking for new things to touch or see. They could be the toddler who wants to open every cabinet (with supervision for safety) or poke at anything unfamiliar. This can lead to extra work for parents or caregivers who need to keep them safe without quashing their spirit.

Energy and Playfulness
Young Sagittarians often have plenty of energy. They may play actively, enjoying games that involve running, climbing, or playing outdoors. They might prefer open-ended toys that let them explore freely, rather than toys with only one method of use. Parents might notice that these children get bored with repetitive activities quickly.

Social Interactions

In playgroups or with siblings, Sagittarius toddlers can be friendly but also direct. They might come across as bold or even bossy at times, not realizing how to share or take turns. Patience and gentle guidance can help them learn these social skills. Because they often speak their mind (as soon as they learn enough words), they might need reminders about politeness and waiting for their turn to talk.

Early School Years (Roughly Ages 6-10)

Hunger for Learning

Once they can read or do basic school tasks, Sagittarius kids can light up when a subject interests them. They might devour books on animals, space, or geography. However, if a lesson feels too slow or repetitive, they may lose focus. Teachers and parents can keep them engaged by offering variety—short, interesting topics, or chances to ask questions and share findings.

Honesty and Friendship

Sagittarius children at this age can be quite open about their likes and dislikes. With friends, they are often cheerful and quick to propose group games. They might also speak bluntly, saying exactly what is on their mind, which can unintentionally hurt classmates' feelings. Guiding them to phrase thoughts more gently helps them develop stronger friendships.

Energy Management

These children may want to run around during breaks, join sports, or do active things after school. Sitting at a desk for long periods could be challenging. Letting them burn off energy in healthy ways—like short breaks or after-school activities—can improve their focus and mood. They usually thrive when given at least some choice in how they spend free time.

Preteen Stage (Roughly Ages 11-12)

Emerging Independence
Around preteen years, Sagittarius kids might show a growing desire for independence. They might want to handle certain tasks themselves, like choosing their outfits or deciding how to organize their schedule. While they still need guidance, giving them small freedoms can help them feel trusted.

Broadening Interests
As they learn more about the world, they may develop broad interests. They could explore science clubs, language lessons, or creative pursuits like drawing or music. Because of their wide curiosity, they might juggle multiple activities. Parents may need to ensure they do not get overwhelmed. A balance of exploration and rest can help them avoid burnout.

Social Life and Group Projects
Preteens often form tighter social circles. A Sagittarius preteen might be at ease in group projects, offering ideas openly. However, they could get restless if the project is too repetitive. Encouraging them to take on roles that involve new thinking or presentation can keep them motivated. They might also help shy classmates speak up, thanks to their friendly manner.

Teenage Years (Roughly Ages 13-18)

Personal Identity and Expression
Teenagers often try to define who they are. A Sagittarius teen might experiment with different styles, friend groups, or interests. They might switch from writing poetry one month to joining a sports club the next. This is a normal part of their quest to see what feels right. Parents can offer support by showing genuine interest and asking thoughtful questions about each new pursuit.

Desire for Freedom
During high school, Sagittarians may voice a strong need for personal freedom. They might want to make more decisions about where they go, how they spend their time, or what they wear. If they feel restricted by too many rules, they might push back. Clear communication from parents—explaining rules that are for safety or fairness—can reduce conflict.

Honesty and Peer Pressure
A Sagittarius teen is likely to speak out against what they see as unfair. They might stand up for friends who are being treated poorly. On the flip side, they can also be tempted by new experiences, occasionally diving into something risky without thinking. Supportive guidance at home—like open talks about peer pressure and consequences—helps them handle these situations wisely.

School Challenges
Some Sagittarians excel if the subjects interest them, but they might struggle in classes that feel dull. Finding ways to connect the class topic to something they value can spark their interest. For instance, if they dislike math but love sports, linking math to sports statistics might help. Teachers who show the broader purpose behind lessons can keep them motivated.

Early Adulthood (Roughly Ages 19-29)

Exploring Career or Higher Education
After high school, a Sagittarius might look for a job, go to college, or pick a training path that allows them to keep learning in a hands-on way. They might switch majors or jobs if they feel bored, searching for a role that fits their energetic, curious nature. They could do well in roles that involve travel, creativity, or social interaction.

Living Arrangements
When living on their own or with roommates, a Sagittarius in their

twenties might enjoy rearranging their space often or bringing in colorful decor. They generally dislike overly strict house rules. If they share housing, they need to compromise, respecting others' routines even if they themselves prefer spontaneity.

Friendship Circles

Sagittarius folks in this age range often have a wide friend network. They might connect with peers who share interests—from sports to volunteer work to music. With new technology and social platforms, they can keep in touch with a broad range of people. However, they must remember that real-life meetups also matter. Balancing online chats and face-to-face time is key.

Managing Money and Routine

Because they like to be flexible, some Sagittarians in early adulthood might find budgeting and stable routines challenging. They might spend on experiences, like concerts or short trips, and forget to put aside savings. Learning basic money skills—like setting up a simple budget—can help them avoid stress. They should aim for some structure while still maintaining their free spirit.

Establishing Adulthood (Roughly Ages 30–40)

Deepening Career Paths

By their thirties, many Sagittarians start to refine their focus. After trying different roles in their twenties, they may settle into a path that offers enough variety while still giving them a sense of stability. For instance, they might become a teacher who can bring new methods to the classroom, or a sales representative who travels to meet clients.

Balancing Freedom and Responsibility

At this stage, responsibilities often increase—like home ownership, long-term relationships, or caring for children. A Sagittarius might worry about losing personal independence. Striking a balance is vital. If they have a family, they can still find ways to keep life interesting, such as planning fun weekend activities or introducing children to new subjects.

Ongoing Learning
Sagittarians do not lose their thirst for knowledge just because they are older. They might take short courses, learn a craft, or explore online classes in fields like tech, design, or health. They often enjoy conferences or local events that discuss big ideas. This keeps them inspired and growing.

Maintaining Social Ties
Friend circles might change as people move away or form families, but Sagittarius usually stays in touch, at least casually. They might gather friends for backyard get-togethers or group trips. If they have children, they could arrange playful activities that also teach something, like a simple science experiment or an outdoor game that introduces new facts.

Midlife (Roughly Ages 40–50)

Reflection and Goals
In their forties or fifties, Sagittarians might start reflecting on what they have achieved and what they still want to explore. Some might realize they want a new career direction. Others might think about ways to help their community or share their knowledge.

Family and Personal Projects
If they have older children, they might guide them with positivity, encouraging them to find their own interests. A Sagittarius in midlife might also start personal projects, like writing a book of short observations, learning new technology, or picking up a skill they never had time for before. They still need mental stimulation to feel fulfilled.

Health and Activity
Physical energy can remain strong if they look after themselves. Sagittarians often do well with routines that mix moderate exercise and creative hobbies. They might avoid overly rigid fitness programs, preferring varied activities they can adapt from day to day. Checking in with a doctor or nutrition expert ensures they keep up healthy habits as they move through midlife changes.

Deeper Friendships
By this age, many Sagittarians value genuine connections over large but shallow networks. They might maintain a handful of core friends who have stood by them. They still enjoy meeting new people, yet they also appreciate the comfort of those who understand them well. Sometimes, they become mentors for younger Sagittarians or others who need advice on how to keep an upbeat attitude.

Later Adulthood (Roughly Ages 50+)

Wisdom and Teaching
Older Sagittarians often delight in sharing lessons they have learned. They might help guide community groups, volunteer in programs that encourage knowledge, or simply be the go-to person for younger relatives seeking advice. They keep their curious mind active by reading, discussing current events, or traveling if possible.

Adapting to Slower Pace
Physical limitations can appear with age, but Sagittarius usually tries to stay lively in spirit. If certain active pursuits become harder, they might switch to gentler ones—like nature walks rather than intense hikes, or low-impact workouts instead of high-energy sports. Mental activities, such as puzzles or writing, can replace some physical activities while still keeping their mind engaged.

Family Role
If they have grandchildren, they might share funny stories, read

interesting books, and spark kids' curiosity about the wider world. They can be the playful grandparent who organizes small games or encourages the children to ask "why?" about everything they see. This can form a warm bond across generations.

Social Involvement

Many Sagittarians remain social even in older age, whether that means leading discussion clubs, attending local events, or hosting small gatherings. If health or mobility issues limit them, they might stay connected through phone calls or online groups. Their positive viewpoint often draws people to them, leading them to form friendships with all age ranges.

Overcoming Age-Related Challenges

Dealing With Routines

At any age, Sagittarians may resist routines. However, as they grow older, medical appointments, financial planning, or family needs can require set schedules. Balancing this with their dislike of being pinned down can be tricky. Finding small ways to add variety—like changing the route to the clinic or listening to exciting audio while handling bills—can make routines less dull.

Emotional Shifts

Life experiences bring joys and sorrows, from triumphs at work to losses in the family. Sagittarians, known for their optimism, might try to brush aside grief, but eventually, they may need to confront it. Learning healthy coping methods—like talking to trusted friends, writing thoughts in a journal, or seeking professional support—can keep them emotionally balanced.

Staying Curious

One of the greatest strengths of Sagittarius is the ability to stay interested in things. This can keep them feeling young, no matter their actual age. Whether learning a new language at 60 or exploring social media at 70, they often keep up with the times. This helps them remain connected to younger generations and relevant topics, preventing feelings of isolation.

Sagittarius Traits in Different Family Roles

Sagittarius as a Parent

Sagittarius parents often encourage their children to explore, ask questions, and stay active. They may bring a fun energy to family life, planning interactive games or outings. However, they need to remember that children also benefit from stability. A little structure can help kids feel secure. By blending freedom with basic rules, a Sagittarius parent can raise confident children who love to learn.

Sagittarius as a Sibling

As a sibling, Sagittarius can be the fun companion who suggests new activities. However, if rules at home conflict with a Sagittarius teen's desire for independence, siblings might see them as unpredictable. Communication can help. Explaining to siblings why they want space or new experiences can foster understanding. They can also learn from siblings who have different approaches.

Sagittarius as a Grandparent or Elder Relative

In older age, a Sagittarius relative might share stories of past events, weaving in humor and lessons learned. Grandchildren might love hearing about the interesting experiences their grandparent had. The younger generation can benefit from the older Sagittarius's advice, which usually comes with a bright perspective. At the same time, the older Sagittarius should remember to listen to younger family members' views, staying updated with modern ways.

Values That Remain Constant With Age

While behaviors adjust over time, certain core values of Sagittarius often remain steady:

Love of Knowledge: Sagittarians rarely stop exploring ideas. Even small changes in technology or new information can spark their interest.

Honesty: They keep a straightforward edge, although they might learn to phrase things more kindly as they mature.

Optimism: Despite ups and downs, they often try to see a bright side or a lesson in challenges.

Freedom: At every stage, they dislike feeling trapped. Even older Sagittarians try to keep a sense of choice, whether it is picking a new hobby or deciding how to spend their free time.

Generosity: Many Sagittarians enjoy sharing insights or supporting friends and family. This can involve simple gifts, time, or encouragement.

Personal Growth Strategies for Different Ages

Because Sagittarians evolve at each stage, here are some growth ideas they can apply as they grow older:

Childhood: Practice sharing and listening to others, working on patience, and learning to handle routines without losing excitement.

Teenage Years: Balance boldness with caution, especially when offered risky choices. Explore many interests but aim to complete important tasks.

20s: Try out different jobs or fields to discover real passions, but keep a basic plan for money and responsibilities.

30s: Aim for a stable path that still includes enough variety. If raising a family, show them the world in small ways while respecting each person's pace.

40s–50s: Reflect on achievements and set fresh goals. Remain curious about new skills or community roles. Keep your social circle strong.

60s and Beyond: Continue learning, stay active within your limits, and share knowledge with younger folks. Embrace the wisdom you have gained while staying open to fresh perspectives.

Handling Midlife or Later-Life Changes

As Sagittarians move through midlife, changes like adjusting to an empty nest or shifting careers can stir up restlessness. They might wonder if they have done enough or if there are new horizons to seek. Here are ways to handle such changes:

Find Meaningful Interests: Pick up a hobby or project that uses your curiosity. This could be digital photography, local history research, or learning a new language.

Mentor Others: Sharing knowledge with younger people can give a sense of purpose, while also renewing your own energy.

Plan for Future Adventures: Even if you cannot be as impulsive as before, small getaways or group activities can bring back the spark of exploration.

Technology and Sagittarius at Different Ages

Sagittarians often adapt well to technology at any age, because it opens doors to information and social connections. Young Sagittarians might use apps to learn or interact with friends. Those in their thirties or forties might embrace digital tools for work. Older Sagittarians can use video calls, online courses, or forums to stay engaged. The common thread is the love of discovering something fresh, and technology can deliver that daily if used mindfully.

Building Legacy and Passing on Wisdom

Later in life, some Sagittarians think about how to pass on their knowledge and experiences. They might write short essays about what they have learned, record family stories, or volunteer in places where they can teach. This desire to share can be fulfilling, helping them leave a positive mark on those around them.

Whether they do this formally—like teaching classes—or informally—like chatting with neighbors—they usually find satisfaction in spreading hope, curiosity, and direct honesty. Younger relatives or community members often value this wisdom, especially when it is given with a touch of humor and warmth.

Self-Care at All Ages

Throughout the years, self-care remains important. Sagittarians might get so involved in projects or social events that they forget to rest. Some self-care tips:

Youth: Set aside calm moments each day, even if just for a short reading break or a quiet walk.

Teens: Handle stress by balancing school, hobbies, and downtime. Talk to trusted folks if pressures build up.

Adults: Incorporate short breaks into busy days—maybe a quick stretch or a simple fun activity.

Midlife: Remember physical health checkups, mental relaxation, and social time. Keep your mind sharp with puzzles, learning, or mild physical exercises.

Spiritual or Philosophical Growth

Many Sagittarians, regardless of age, enjoy exploring philosophical ideas or big questions about life. This can lead them to read about different beliefs, attend talks, or have deep conversations. Some might find comfort in a spiritual group, while others keep a personal practice, such as quiet reflection or mindful observation of nature. As they get older, these practices can help them stay grounded and find meaning beyond daily tasks.

Maintaining Friendships Across Decades

One of the joys of Sagittarius is their ability to keep up connections across long periods. They might have childhood friends they still chat with or new friends they discover in unexpected places. Because they are open and good at conversation, many Sagittarians can maintain a network that spans multiple generations or backgrounds. This diversity of friendships keeps their outlook fresh and prevents a feeling of stagnation.

Facing Life's Challenges With Optimism

At every age, challenges such as setbacks, grief, or health issues can arise. Sagittarians often respond initially with positivity. However, if the issue is deeper, they might need extra support to face it fully rather than brushing it off. Talking to counselors, joining support groups, or simply sharing with a trusted friend can help them cope in a balanced manner. Maintaining hope is good, but pairing hope with action and understanding is even better.

Enjoying Hobbies and Leisure Over Time

A Sagittarius might find that certain pastimes follow them through life. For instance, if they loved reading about faraway lands as a child, they may turn this into actual travel experiences as adults, and then perhaps into writing stories or blogs in older age. Each stage allows them to see the hobby from a new angle. By staying open to how they can tweak or expand these interests, Sagittarians keep the excitement alive.

Avoiding the Trap of Overextension

Because they have a broad range of interests, Sagittarians can sometimes spread themselves too thin. At any age, learning to say "no" to too many commitments is important. They should pick a few areas that truly matter instead of trying to do everything at once. This prevents exhaustion and allows them to focus on quality over quantity, whether at work, home, or in social activities.

Embracing Each Stage With Confidence

Sagittarius energy evolves, but the core traits—optimism, curiosity, and the need for some level of personal freedom—remain. Embracing these traits at each life stage can help Sagittarians feel authentic. They do not have to mimic someone else's idea of how to be a child, teen, adult, or elder. Instead, they can adapt their natural traits in ways that suit their responsibilities and relationships.

Lifelong Learning Approach

One standout feature of Sagittarius is lifelong learning. They might do the following at different stages:

Childhood: Ask endless "why" questions or read about fascinating topics.

Teenage Years: Join clubs, explore online tutorials, or watch educational channels.

Adulthood: Attend seminars, try new job skills, read up on diverse subjects.

Elder Years: Share knowledge, read widely, keep up with societal changes.

This approach helps them remain mentally sharp and excited about what lies ahead. Being a "student of life" suits a Sagittarius from young to old.

Adapting When Freedom Is Limited

Not all situations allow for full freedom. Some might face strict workplaces, health restrictions, or caring for a loved one. In these scenarios, Sagittarians can focus on small freedoms—choosing little treats or scheduling short breaks. They might also find ways to incorporate variety, such as changing up routines in minor ways or watching interesting documentaries to feed their mind. By seeking small outlets for their free spirit, they can stay positive even in limiting times.

CHAPTER 13: SIBLINGS & FAMILY

Family life is an important environment for everyone, and Sagittarius individuals often bring their own spark to that setting. In this chapter, we will focus on how Sagittarius behaves and feels within the family, especially in sibling relationships. We will introduce fresh insights about how a Sagittarius child, teen, or adult interacts with family members, how parents can understand a Sagittarius child, and how siblings can get along better. We will avoid repeating details already covered in previous chapters, keeping our focus on new, in-depth knowledge about family connections for Sagittarius.

Sagittarius as a Young Sibling

When a Sagittarius is a younger sibling in the family, they tend to look up to their older siblings with a curious, wide-eyed interest. Even at an early age, they might want to explore the older siblings' rooms or try to copy what they see them doing. Sometimes, they ask direct questions that catch the older siblings off-guard: "Why do you do that?" or "Why can't I stay up late too?" Their direct way of speaking can be fun, but it may also cause small quarrels if the older sibling wants privacy.

Balancing Curiosity and Respect

Respecting Boundaries: Young Sagittarius siblings should learn early that being curious is good, but everyone deserves some personal space. If an older sibling has items they do not want touched, or times they want to be alone, a Sagittarius child can be guided to understand that it is not rejection; it is simply part of growing up.

Sharing Interests: An older sibling can also benefit by sharing certain activities. For instance, if the older sibling has a favorite simple game or puzzle, letting the Sagittarius child join (in a limited way) can satisfy that curiosity without crossing boundaries too much.

Handling Energy Levels

Sagittarius children might have a lot of energy. They could run around the house, making the older sibling feel pestered. Encouraging outside play, or setting up a safe space inside where the Sagittarius child can move around, helps them release that energy without constantly pushing into the older sibling's personal area.

Sagittarius as an Older Sibling

When a Sagittarius is the older sibling, they bring a fun and upbeat spirit to the family dynamic. They often enjoy teaching their younger siblings interesting things, whether it is a new board game, a silly dance, or random facts about animals. However, they might also have a restless streak that makes them move on quickly from one activity to another.

Being a Guide

Leading By Example: Younger siblings often watch what older ones do. A Sagittarius older sibling can show confidence and an open mind, which might inspire the younger ones to explore new hobbies or books. At the same time, if the Sagittarius teen frequently changes interests, the younger sibling might feel confused about following along.

Watching Out for Tact: Because of the Sagittarius trait of direct speech, an older Sagittarius sibling might correct a younger one too bluntly. They can learn to phrase things kindly, especially if the younger child is sensitive. A small shift in wording—"Let's try it this way, it might work better," instead of "You're doing it all wrong"—can keep the bond strong.

Shared Activities

One benefit of having a Sagittarius as an older sibling is that they usually enjoy fun outings and open-ended activities. They might take their younger sibling to the backyard to explore, or set up a pretend fort in the living room. These spontaneous moments can bring joy and help both siblings connect on a level that is both playful and supportive.

Sagittarius and Sibling Rivalries

Sibling rivalry can happen in any family, but Sagittarius siblings might respond in particular ways due to their direct nature. If they feel they are not given enough space, or if they think the rules are too tight, they might speak out in ways that ruffle feathers. On the flip side, a Sagittarius sibling could also be the peacemaker if they choose to step in with a positive angle.

Common Causes of Conflict

Need for Freedom: If a Sagittarius feels another sibling is too controlling or bossy, they might snap back with blunt comments.

Honest Opinions: They could say something that hurts a sibling's feelings, even if they did not intend to cause harm.

Different Energies: A quiet sibling might be annoyed by the Sagittarius sibling's energy, while the Sagittarius sibling feels the quiet one is too dull.

Conflict Resolution Tips

Allow Cool-Down Time: Because Sagittarius can respond quickly when upset, giving each sibling a short break to calm down can prevent arguments from escalating.

Encourage Fair Talk: If a Sagittarius sibling has strong opinions, parents or other family members can guide them to use fair language ("I feel..." rather than "You always...").

Celebrate Strengths Together: By highlighting what each sibling does well, the family can create a space where Sagittarius's free spirit is admired, and the sibling's qualities are also valued, reducing comparisons and jealousy.

Sagittarius as a Child in the Family

Outside of sibling relationships, the Sagittarius child typically has certain patterns when dealing with parents, grandparents, or other close relatives. They might bring enthusiasm to everyday tasks, but also question rules or feel impatient if the family schedule is too rigid.

Communication with Parents

Curiosity: Sagittarius children often ask direct questions about why the family does things a certain way. They might not accept "Because I said so" as a response. Explaining the reasons behind rules or chores can help them feel more cooperative.

Honesty: These children will usually let parents know if they dislike something. Parents can encourage them to express disagreements politely. This develops healthier communication in the long run.

Family Activities

Outdoor Fun: A Sagittarius child is likely to enjoy family picnics, simple sports, or day trips to interesting locations. They usually do well in places that allow some freedom of movement.

Creative Projects: They may also want to try new crafts or household science experiments, as variety keeps them engaged. Parents can rotate these activities so the Sagittarius child does not become bored.

Discipline and Guidance

Respecting Boundaries: Because of their energetic nature, Sagittarius children may push limits. Parents can set clear, fair rules, and explain why those limits exist. This helps the child feel that the boundaries are not just random.

Natural Consequences: Instead of harsh punishments, letting the Sagittarius child see the result of their choices can be effective. For instance, if they forget to do a chore, they might lose some free time to fix the oversight. This teaches responsibility without stifling their spirit.

Sagittarius Teens in the Family

When Sagittarius individuals reach their teenage years, the family dynamic can shift noticeably. Their need for independence grows, and they might be impatient with routines that they see as dull. They could push back on curfews or rules they consider too strict.

Encouraging Freedom Within Limits

Open Discussions: Parents can set boundaries in a calm, logical way, allowing the Sagittarius teen to ask questions. The teen might be more likely to respect rules if they see the reasoning behind them, such as safety concerns.

Positive Challenges: Sagittarius teens might respond well to tasks that let them use their imagination or leadership abilities. For example, allowing them to plan a small family activity (like picking a movie or creating a weekend schedule) can fulfill their desire for autonomy while teaching them to handle responsibility.

Emotional Support

Handling Blunt Talk: When teens are in a mood, their speech can be extra direct. Family members should remain calm, encouraging them to phrase concerns respectfully. At the same time, it is vital not to punish them simply for being honest.

Listening to Big Ideas: Sagittarius teens may bring home a new idea or project every week. Rather than dismiss these as "just a phase," family members can show interest. Asking polite questions can support the teen's exploration without making them feel restricted.

Sagittarius Parents

Fast-forward to when a Sagittarius becomes a parent. They often want to share their love of variety and open-minded thinking with their children. They might organize playful at-home experiments or read interesting books together. They try to encourage a sense of wonder in the kids. Yet, challenges can appear when it comes to structure and routines.

Parenting Style

Encouraging Exploration: A Sagittarius parent usually wants their children to try different hobbies or read about different topics. This can lead to well-rounded kids who are not afraid to ask questions.

Moderate Rules: Because they dislike strictness themselves, Sagittarius parents might set fewer rules. However, children do need some order for safety and predictability. A good balance might be a short list of major house rules, paired with freedoms in smaller areas (like choosing after-school activities).

Balancing Fun and Duty

Responsibility Lessons: Even though a Sagittarius parent wants children to enjoy exploring, they also need to ensure the kids learn about responsibilities—cleaning up, being polite, and handling tasks. Sagittarius parents can link responsibilities to fun. For instance, if chores are done, the child gets to pick a simple game to play as a reward.

Leading by Example: Children might watch how the parent reacts when bored or frustrated. If the Sagittarius parent shows healthy ways of dealing with those feelings—like taking a short break or doing something creative—the children can learn valuable coping techniques.

Extended Family Connections

Sagittarians often value a wide social circle, which can include extended family—grandparents, aunts, uncles, or cousins. They might be the family member who proposes a gathering, or who keeps up with relatives through phone calls or messages. Yet, they can also feel restless if extended family events are too formal or full of small talk.

Strategies for Harmony

Short and Engaging Visits: If gatherings last many hours with little variety, a Sagittarius might get fidgety. Suggesting a casual group activity—like a group game or a shared story time—can make extended family events more enjoyable.

Communication with Older Relatives: Sagittarians can show respect by genuinely listening to older family members' stories. They might even learn interesting historical facts or life lessons. In turn, they can share their own experiences or new knowledge, bridging the age gap with curiosity and warmth.

Passing on Traditions (With a Twist)

Some families have long-standing customs. Sagittarians may be okay with these as long as they see the meaning behind them. If they feel a tradition is just "forced," they might lose interest. Talking to older relatives about the history or background can help the Sagittarius family member engage more. They might even suggest a fresh spin on an old custom—keeping it relevant and enjoyable without discarding it entirely.

Multi-Generational Households

In some families, grandparents, parents, and children live under one roof. A Sagittarius in this setup might need extra patience, since multiple generations can have conflicting schedules and rules.

Understanding Different Generations

Grandparents' Pace: Older family members might move more slowly or like routines. The Sagittarius might find it hard to adapt to a regimented schedule. But by having open conversations, they can learn how certain routines give comfort to the older relatives.

Role of the Sagittarius: They can bring positive energy, especially if the household feels dull. Suggesting small shared moments—like reading a short story together or going out for a brief walk—can brighten everyone's day. Meanwhile, they can also learn from the wisdom of grandparents.

Avoiding Overwhelm

Finding Personal Space: In a busy household, the Sagittarius might feel cramped. Having a corner of the home where they can read or think quietly helps. They can also step outside for a brief stroll if they need a breather.

Respecting Privacy for Others: If grandparents or younger siblings want quiet time, the Sagittarius should learn to dial back the energy level. This fosters more harmony overall.

Supportive Family Roles for Sagittarius

Sagittarius members can contribute greatly to a supportive family environment, thanks to their open-mindedness and eagerness to try new things. Here are some ways they can strengthen the family bond:

Organizing Lighthearted Activities: Whether it is a simple board game night or a weekend backyard session, Sagittarius can be the motivator who keeps family fun on the schedule.

Sharing Positive Views: When others feel down, a friendly pep talk from the Sagittarius can remind them of the bright side. As long as they remain mindful of deeper concerns, their optimism can uplift family members.

Encouraging Ongoing Learning: They might introduce the family to documentaries, articles, or short lessons that spark fresh ideas. This broadens horizons and makes conversation more interesting.

Challenges Sagittarius Faces in the Family

While they have strengths, Sagittarians also face certain challenges in family life. Recognizing these can help them navigate issues more gracefully:

Impatience with Routine: Repetitive chores and daily tasks can make them restless. They might need strategies to make these tasks feel less stale.

Blunt Comments: Their direct words can sting sensitive family members, leading to hurt feelings or arguments.

Commitment Struggles: Sometimes, they start family projects (like planning an event or remodeling a space) with enthusiasm but lose interest halfway. This can frustrate siblings or parents who rely on them to finish.

Wanting Space in a Busy Household: Family demands may conflict with their need for alone time or flexible schedules.

Communication Tips for Sagittarius Within the Family

To handle potential rough spots, Sagittarians can refine their communication:

Listen Actively: Even if they have a quick solution, pausing to let a family member share their full thoughts can prevent misunderstandings.

Use "I" Statements: When disagreeing, say "I feel..." or "I think..." rather than "You always..." or "You never..." This approach focuses on their viewpoint without attacking.

Offer Explanations: If they want to skip a family event or do something alone, explaining the reason kindly can reduce confusion or hurt. "I need some quiet time to recharge" can be better than just disappearing.

Encouraging Mutual Respect

For a healthy family life, mutual respect goes both ways. The Sagittarius can help foster this by:

Respecting Schedules: If a family meal is at 6 PM, trying to show up on time shows respect for others' planning.

Accepting Different Preferences: A sibling might hate loud music, so the Sagittarius can use headphones. Or a parent might need the house to be calm after a certain hour. By adapting, the Sagittarius shows consideration.

Seeking Solutions Together: If a conflict arises, focusing on, "How can we fix this for everyone?" is more productive than blaming.

Building Better Bonds Over Time

Sagittarius family members often deepen their ties with siblings or parents as the years pass. Early clashes can mellow if everyone learns how to handle the Sagittarius traits—both positive and challenging. Over time, the family might see the Sagittarius individual as a source of upbeat energy and fresh ideas.

Shared Routines (With Flexibility): Planning a weekly dinner but allowing the Sagittarius to pick a new recipe or theme can combine stability with variety.

Celebrating Differences: Family can point out strengths in each person. One sibling might excel at organizing, another might excel at creative tasks, and the Sagittarius might excel at bringing a new angle or humor. Recognizing these different strengths reduces comparisons and builds unity.

Coping with Serious Family Issues

At times, serious family matters—such as illnesses, financial problems, or losses—can arise. A Sagittarius might try to keep spirits high, but they also need to acknowledge real sadness or worry:

Balancing Positivity and Empathy: While staying upbeat is good, the Sagittarius should offer genuine listening to those who are upset. If a parent is grieving, for example, endless jokes might feel insensitive.

Pitching In: If chores or tasks build up because of a major issue, this is a moment for the Sagittarius to show commitment. Helping consistently, rather than losing focus, can provide real support.

Seeking Outside Assistance: Sometimes, professional advice or counseling is needed. A Sagittarius who remains open to this can help the entire family handle the situation with less stress.

Multi-Household Families and Sagittarius

In modern times, families might be spread across different homes due to separation, divorce, or other factors. A Sagittarius living part-time in two households might adapt quickly, as they enjoy variety. However, they can also feel conflicted if the rules differ greatly. They might get restless moving from one environment to another.

Tips for Multi-Household Situations

Clear Communication: If the Sagittarius is old enough, letting them express which rules or schedules make sense can reduce friction. Parents can work on consistency or at least explain differences kindly.

Carrying Personal Items: A Sagittarius might keep a "comfort kit" of small items (books, mementos, or creative tools) that move with them. This helps them feel at home in both places.

Staying Connected: If siblings are split between households, the Sagittarius might use calls or texts to keep up daily contact, preserving that sibling bond.

Adult Sagittarius and Elderly Family Members

When Sagittarians become adults, they might have aging parents or grandparents who need help. Their open nature can be a great asset in staying connected. However, they should be mindful of how to balance their busy or flexible lifestyle with the steadiness that older relatives might need.

Frequent but Adaptable Visits: Scheduling short, more frequent visits can maintain a bond without making the Sagittarius feel trapped. Bringing a bit of positivity—like interesting stories or showing them new technology—can brighten an elder's day.

Respecting Limits: Elders might move slowly or have health concerns. A Sagittarius adult can slow their usual pace to match their loved one's comfort level, showing empathy.

Family Gatherings Led by Sagittarius

If a Sagittarius likes to plan gatherings or get-togethers for the whole family, they can put their creativity to good use:

Varying the Themes: Instead of doing the exact same meal or activity every time, they might mix it up: one time a casual outdoor meet, the next time a potluck with different cuisines.

Setting Relaxed Rules: A few small guidelines (like what time it starts, or what dishes people bring) can help the event run smoothly. But not going overboard with strictness suits a Sagittarius's style.

Inviting Input: They can ask family members for suggestions, ensuring everyone feels included. This approach builds cooperation instead of letting the Sagittarius run the entire show solo.

Handling Criticism from Family

Family members sometimes criticize each other's choices. A Sagittarius might face comments such as "Why can't you stick to one plan?" or "You always change your mind." Because Sagittarians care about personal freedom, these remarks can sting.

Strategies for Taking Feedback

Acknowledge Concerns: Even if the criticism feels unfair, acknowledging the family member's worry can open dialogue. "I see you're worried about my changing plans often."

Share Your Perspective: Explain why you need flexibility. If the family member understands your reasons, they might accept it more.

Decide If Changes Are Needed: If the feedback points out a genuine issue (like forgetting to pay bills or leaving tasks half-finished), then using a basic system—like a checklist—might help.

Emotional Health in the Sagittarius Household

Sagittarius family members can bring laughter and a "can-do" attitude, but they also need space to process tougher emotions. If a child or sibling is feeling down, the Sagittarius must be careful not to dismiss it with a quick "It'll be fine." Sometimes deeper listening is required.

Encouraging Heartfelt Chats: Set aside times to talk without distractions, maybe after dinner or on a quiet weekend afternoon.

Balancing Humor: Jokes can lighten tension, but if someone is truly upset, a Sagittarius should hold back on humor until the person feels heard.

Parenting a Sagittarius Child

If you are a parent of a Sagittarius child, here are a few tips to keep your relationship constructive and warm:

Give Them Choices: Let them pick from a few suitable options. This makes them feel involved rather than controlled.

Explain the "Why" Behind Rules: Sagittarians often respond better when they see logical reasons, not just commands.

Encourage Their Curiosity: If they latch onto an interesting topic, help them find books, videos, or clubs that support it.

Reward Consistency: Praise them when they follow through on tasks, reinforcing the idea that staying committed pays off.

Model Calm Speech: If they get blunt, show them how to phrase concerns kindly. Children often learn by watching how adults talk.

Healing Family Tensions

If a Sagittarius has had conflicts with a sibling or parent over time, healing may involve:

Honest Conversations: A well-timed talk, where both sides share grievances without interruption, can clear the air.

Small Gestures of Kindness: Sending a supportive message or offering help can show you value the relationship.

Agreeing on Limits: If certain topics always cause fights, maybe set them aside for a while until trust grows stronger.

Sagittarius can use their ability to see possibilities to imagine a better path forward. They just need the patience to work through older hurts.

Sagittarius as a Family Peacemaker

In some families, Sagittarians step up as peacemakers when arguments arise. Their willingness to talk openly can help. They might:

Listen to All Sides: Hear each person's viewpoint.

Offer Fresh Solutions: Suggest a compromise that no one considered before.

Maintain Positivity: While not downplaying serious issues, they can remind everyone that a resolution is possible if they stay calm.

This role suits Sagittarians if they remember to be respectful to each viewpoint, rather than pushing only their own ideas.

Blending Different Personalities at Home

Many families include siblings or parents with varied zodiac signs (as discussed in Chapter 11). A Sagittarius living with a more cautious sign, like Taurus or Cancer, might find it tricky at first. But they can blend successfully by:

Being Patient with Slower Rhythms: Understand that not everyone leaps into activities quickly.

Accepting Emotional Depth: If someone needs more heartfelt talks, the Sagittarius can provide that space.

Using Differences as Strengths: If a sibling is detail-oriented, pair that with the Sagittarius's creative approach to chores or shared projects.

Passing on Traditions and Values

Even though Sagittarius might have a modern or flexible outlook, they can still keep family values alive. It's about finding ways to adapt. For instance, if the family has a yearly special meal, the Sagittarius can add a twist to the recipes or help set up a relaxed mood. Maintaining a link to heritage can help siblings and relatives feel grounded while still giving room for fun changes.

CHAPTER 14: FUN ACTIVITIES FOR SAGITTARIUS

Sagittarius individuals are known for their bright spirit and eagerness to try different things. They often enjoy activities that spark curiosity, test their energy, or let them learn something new. In this chapter, we will explore a wide range of fun options that can appeal to Sagittarius across different ages. We will steer clear of repeating earlier content and give fresh ideas that match a Sagittarius's natural inclinations. Whether you are a Sagittarius looking for new pastimes or a friend or family member hoping to plan something that will excite a Sagittarius, these suggestions can help keep life engaging and lively.

Outdoor Exploration

Many Sagittarians enjoy being outside because it provides a sense of open space and fresh air. Some possible activities:

Nature Trails: Walking along scenic paths, noticing plants and small wildlife. A Sagittarius might bring a small notebook to jot down interesting observations.

Picnics in the Park: Though simple, a relaxed meal in a green setting can give a Sagittarius a welcome break from routine. If they can bring a Frisbee or a simple ball game, even better.

Star Gazing: At night, finding a spot away from city lights to look at constellations can appeal to a Sagittarius's curiosity about the wider world.

Making It More Exciting

Treasure Hunt: Turning a nature walk into a small treasure hunt by hiding clues can keep a Sagittarius engaged.

Photo Challenge: Bring a camera or phone to snap pictures of unique things—like unusual leaves, rock formations, or cloud shapes.

Creative Arts and Crafts

Sagittarians often like trying creative outlets, even if they are not experts. They value experiences that let them express ideas or just have fun with color and design.

Tie-Dye: Dying T-shirts or cloth with bright colors can be a lively project. The final result might be unpredictable, which adds to the fun.

Collage Making: Using old magazines or printed photos, a Sagittarius can craft a board that reflects their interests—favorite quotes, images of places they want to see, or silly pictures.

DIY Projects: Building a simple shelf, painting a piece of furniture, or making homemade decorations can feed their need for hands-on variety.

Group vs. Solo

Group Workshop: If they want social interaction, a local craft workshop could be perfect.

Solo Experimenting: If they want time alone, setting up a corner at home with supplies can let them explore at their own pace without pressure.

Cultural and Global Interests

Because Sagittarius often enjoys learning about different places and customs, they might take pleasure in activities tied to global culture:

International Cooking Night: Try preparing meals from different regions, such as simple noodles from one country or a mild curry from another. Exploring new flavors can spark their interest.

Language Basics: Learning a few key phrases in another language can be exciting. They might watch short online lessons or get a phrasebook.

Documentary Viewing: They can watch short documentaries about interesting cultures, wildlife, or historical sites. Pair this with a snack that fits the theme of the documentary.

Mixing Fun and Knowledge

World Music Playlist: Create a playlist with songs from around the globe, letting the Sagittarius discover new rhythms.

Local Cultural Events: If the community hosts cultural fairs or festivals, attending can let them see unique performances and crafts.

Indoor Games and Challenges

When the weather is not ideal or if they want a cozy indoor experience, Sagittarians can still find plenty of exciting pursuits:

Board Games with Strategy: They might enjoy games that involve some tactics or quick thinking, but not ones that are so complex they become tedious. Examples include card-based games that require clever moves.

Escape Room at Home: Setting up an escape room scenario with puzzles and clues can be thrilling. Sagittarians can use their quick minds to solve riddles and find hidden messages.

Group Quiz Night: They can gather friends for a friendly trivia contest, possibly including questions about geography, science, or odd facts. The Sagittarius love of learning will make this a hit.

Staying Motivated

Rotating Themes: Each time, they can choose a new theme, such as science one week or music the next, keeping it fresh.

Small Rewards: Even a fun treat at the end can add a sense of achievement.

Physical Activities and Sports

Sagittarians typically have lively energy, so sports or movement-based activities can keep them interested:

Recreational Team Sports: Soccer, basketball, or even a casual round of badminton can let them burn off restlessness.

Dance Sessions: Whether it is a dance class or just playing upbeat music at home, movement-based activities can raise their spirits.

Light Hiking: While we avoided certain words, a moderate walk on a trail with slight inclines can fit their desire for being active without being overly intense.

Biking in Safe Areas: A Sagittarius can explore nearby paths or quiet roads, observing new sights along the way.

Keeping It Varied

Try Different Sports Periodically: Swapping between sports or exercise routines can fight boredom. One month they might do casual volleyball, another month they try table tennis.

Friendly Competitions: If they like a bit of challenge, mild competitions with friends can add excitement, as long as everyone keeps it light-hearted.

Volunteer and Community Projects

Sagittarians often enjoy feeling that they are part of something bigger. Volunteering can give them a sense of purpose while also letting them learn new skills or meet different people:

Animal Shelter Helper: They can help walk dogs, clean cages, or socialize with cats, providing a direct link to living creatures.

Community Clean-Up: Participating in local trash pick-up events in parks or public spaces can appeal to a Sagittarius's sense of caring about the world.

Youth Program Support: If they are older, they might volunteer to teach basic skills or read stories to younger kids, blending their love of sharing knowledge with community involvement.

Why This Suits Sagittarius

Feeling of Achievement: They see immediate positive results, like a cleaner park or happier animals.

Connection with People: They might meet volunteers from diverse backgrounds, which sparks interesting conversations.

Simple Adventure in Daily Life

Even small changes can feel like an adventure to a Sagittarius if approached with the right mindset:

Unplanned Walk: Heading out without a set path, letting curiosity guide the route.

New Restaurant Exploration: Stopping by a café or diner they have never tried before, sampling a unique item on the menu.

Random Library Visit: Browsing shelves in a random section, picking a book that catches the eye, can feed their mind with unexpected knowledge.

Keeping Spontaneity Safe

Set Basic Limits: For instance, if going on an unplanned walk, ensure they have a charged phone and know the general area so they do not get lost or stuck.

Invite a Friend: Sharing these small adventures can double the fun and help them keep track of time if they have other obligations later.

Mind-Stimulating Hobbies

Sagittarius individuals might appreciate hobbies that make them think deeply or discover interesting facts:

Puzzle Solving: Whether it is crosswords, Sudoku, or logic puzzles, these can be done alone or in groups.

Collecting Odd Facts: Keeping a small notebook or digital note of fun trivia or intriguing info discovered day by day.

Online Discussion Groups: Joining digital communities about science, history, or any topic that sparks curiosity. They can bounce ideas around with like-minded folks around the world.

Avoiding Monotony

Vary Puzzle Types: They can switch between word puzzles, number puzzles, or visual puzzles.

Set Challenges with Friends: They might say, "Let's each find five odd facts about ocean life and share them at the end of the week."

Local Trips

We can say that shorter trips around town or nearby regions can keep a Sagittarius engaged:

Farmers' Markets: Strolling through stalls of fresh produce or handmade goods. They might learn about local farmers or try new flavors.

Museum Day: Checking out exhibits that teach them something fresh—like a science museum or a cultural display.

Historic Town Visits: Many places have small, older towns with interesting buildings, local tales, and cozy shops.

Making It More Interactive

Audio Guides or Apps: Some museums or historic spots offer phone apps or audio tours that give extra stories. This kind of interactive learning suits a Sagittarius mind.

Bring a Sketchbook or Journal: While exploring a new place, they can note down interesting tidbits, draw quick sketches, or collect postcards.

Group Social Nights

Sagittarius folks often enjoy social connections. Organizing group nights with a fun twist can bring people together:

Theme Potluck: Each person brings a dish inspired by a region or a specific type of food. Sagittarius can learn new recipes and flavors.

Talent Share Night: Friends take turns showing a short skill or hobby—like a small magic trick, a poem, or a craft demonstration. A Sagittarius might like to teach something they just discovered.

Movie Discussion Evening: Instead of just watching a film, they can talk about its plot or message afterward, satisfying the Sagittarius taste for sharing opinions.

Keeping It Fresh

Change Themes Regularly: A different theme each time (like international cuisine, local comfort foods, or a color-themed meal) ensures no gathering feels stale.

Invite Varied Personalities: Mixing friends from different backgrounds can lead to lively conversations, which Sagittarius usually appreciates.

Music and Rhythm

Many Sagittarians love music because it taps into emotion and keeps energy levels high:

Instrument Sampling: They could try simple instruments such as a ukulele or a small percussion tool. They do not have to aim for perfection—exploration is enough.

Rhythm Games: Dance-based video games or drumming games can be a way to move and have fun at the same time.

Open Mic Nights: If they have any interest in singing or performing, a relaxed open mic event might let them share their bright spirit without heavy pressure.

Keeping Enthusiasm

Jam Sessions with Friends: Even if they are not pros, a few open-minded pals can gather with simple instruments. The atmosphere is what counts.

Playlist Swaps: Sharing playlists with friends or discovering new global artists can feed Sagittarius's curiosity about different sounds.

Brainstorm and Innovation Activities

Given their fondness for ideas, Sagittarians can thrive in activities that let them solve problems or invent things:

Building Clubs: Local maker spaces or clubs that let people tinker with electronics, robotics, or crafts.

Idea Pitch Groups: Some communities have casual get-togethers where members share a concept and get feedback. Sagittarius's open mind fits right in.

Personal Innovation Projects: At home, they might try to create a new board game, design an app prototype, or come up with a small invention that solves a minor household issue.

Keeping Projects Manageable

Small-Scale Goals: Instead of trying to design a massive invention right away, they can set a modest target. Achieving it keeps the excitement alive.

Partner Up: Partnering with someone detail-oriented can help a Sagittarius get from concept to finished project without losing steam halfway.

Personal Development

While Sagittarians sometimes dislike words like "training" or "lessons," they do enjoy growing their skills and perspective if it feels stimulating:

Short Workshops: Whether it is a photography class, an online course on digital art, or a day session on public speaking, these can suit a Sagittarius's appetite for learning.

Skill Swaps: They can partner with a friend who knows something different—for instance, trading guitar lessons for cooking lessons.

Meditation or Calm Practices: Even though they like being active, short calming exercises can help them handle stress or restlessness.

Finding the Right Approach

Choose Varied Topics: A single long program might bore them. Instead, they could try multiple short ones, each focusing on a unique topic.

Reflect on Progress: Keeping a simple journal can help a Sagittarius see how much they've learned. This encourages them to stick with the activity.

Game Creation

Sagittarians might also love creating their own small games or puzzles to challenge friends:

DIY Card Games: With a stack of blank cards, they can draw or write rules, forming a custom card game.

Scavenger Hunts: Designing clues around the house or yard, with a final prize at the end. This merges creativity with excitement.

Quiz Master Role: They can compile trivia and host a family quiz night. This channels their love of random facts into a shared experience.

Sharing and Evolving the Game

Getting Feedback: Let friends or family try the game and suggest tweaks. The interactive process can be as fun as playing.

Introducing Variation: After each session, the Sagittarius might add or remove rules, making sure it never grows stale.

Travel on a Budget

Long or pricey adventures might be out of reach for some, but Sagittarians can still find ways to broaden their horizons:

Local Day Trips: Checking out lesser-known areas a short drive or bus ride away—like a hidden lake, a small historical site, or a quirky roadside attraction.

House Swaps: If they have friends in different cities, they can arrange to stay at each other's homes for a few days.

Digital Explorations: Using online tools to virtually see famous museums or scenic spots around the globe. They can follow that up by cooking a dish from that area or learning a few cultural facts.

Keeping It Realistic

Saving in Small Steps: Putting aside a little money regularly can fund a local trip or special outing.

Combining Fun with Work: If they must travel for work or study, they can add a day or two of exploration nearby. This way, they merge learning with recreation.

Fostering Friendships Through Shared Activities

Since Sagittarians are sociable, picking activities that allow others to join can enrich their bonds:

Group Hiking: Invite friends for a mild hike, bring snacks, and stop for scenic photos.

Community Challenges: Like a mini marathon or a walkathon for a good cause. Sagittarius can support something meaningful while staying active with friends.

Learning Clubs: Form a small group to read about a topic, try a skill, or watch tutorial videos together. Everyone can share what they learn.

Adding Fun to Friendship

Themed Days: If they meet every Sunday, each friend can propose a theme (like music day, craft day, debate day) so there's always something fresh.

Rotating Leaders: Each friend takes a turn leading the activity, ensuring variety and shared responsibility.

Tech-Related Adventures

If a Sagittarius has a knack for technology, they can explore fun tech activities:

Coding Games: Websites or apps that teach basic coding with playful puzzles.

Virtual Reality Testing: If they have access to VR gear, exploring digital worlds can satisfy curiosity.

Robotics Kits: Building a small robotic vehicle or gadget that can move, beep, or follow commands.

Keeping Tech Balanced

Limit Screen Overload: Setting time boundaries helps prevent them from getting stuck in front of screens for too long. They can still blend physical and outdoor interests alongside tech pursuits.

Invite Collaboration: Working with a friend on a coding project or robot kit can add a social element, which appeals to many Sagittarians.

Gardening with a Twist

While "gardening" might sound slow or routine, Sagittarians can add excitement:

Unusual Plants: Instead of the standard tomatoes or flowers, they might try growing something a bit exotic (as long as it's suited to the local climate).

Mini Herb Box: A small indoor herb box can give quick results. They can use the herbs in cooking experiments, tying two activities together.

Vertical Gardens: If space is tight, a vertical setup on a balcony or a wall can be visually appealing and different from standard ground-level gardening.

Keeping It Interesting

Track Growth: Taking weekly pictures to see how the plants progress can feel like a mini project.

Use the Harvest: If they grow herbs or small veggies, they can try new recipes. That sense of immediate use can keep them motivated.

Small Scientific Experiments

Sagittarians who love to learn might enjoy safe, simple experiments at home:

Kitchen Science: Experiments like making quick dough, seeing how yeast works, or creating a volcano effect with baking soda and vinegar.

Household Physics: Testing which paper airplane design flies the farthest, or exploring how shadows change at different times of day.

Mini Greenhouse in a Jar: Placing seeds and damp cotton in a jar to watch them sprout. Checking daily progress can be rewarding.

Sharing Discoveries

Invite Friends: Doing small experiments together can lead to fun interactions and possible laughs if something goes wrong.

Record Observations: A tiny lab notebook or smartphone notes can make the process feel more official.

Self-Challenges for Mental Growth

Sagittarians might start personal challenges that do not require big investments:

Reading Goals: Decide to read a certain number of books in a month, each on a different topic.

Daily Fact Challenge: Try to learn one new fact every day and share it with someone. This keeps the mind active and fosters interesting chats.

30-Day Creative Spark: Sketch, write a short poem, or take a themed photo every day for a month.

Staying Motivated

Track Progress Visually: A chart or list pinned to a wall can show each day's achievement, giving a sense of steady momentum.

Friendly Accountability: Teaming up with a buddy who also does daily goals helps them stay on course.

Simple Relaxation Ideas

Not all activities have to be high-energy. Some Sagittarians need mellow moments too, as constant activity can wear them out:

Light Yoga or Stretching: Simple routines that do not feel too rigid, yet help them relax their muscles.

Coloring Books for Adults: Adding color to intricate designs can be oddly calming for a Sagittarius mind, especially if they pick vibrant palettes.

Nature Sounds: Listening to recorded sounds of rain or gentle waves can soothe them before bed.

Avoiding Restlessness

Brief Sessions: Keeping relaxing activities under 15 or 20 minutes might suit a Sagittarius who gets antsy if an activity drags on.

Combining Relaxation with Inspiration: For instance, a short guided relaxation followed by a small bit of reading that offers new insights.

Creating a Vision Board

A vision board can be a fun, imaginative activity for a Sagittarius who thinks about what the future might hold:

Collect Images and Quotes: Clip images from magazines or print them out, focusing on places they want to see, subjects they want to learn, or personal aims they find inspiring.

Arrange on a Board or Large Paper: They can group them by category or blend them randomly. The visual mix often sparks new thoughts.

Review Often: By looking at the board now and then, they remind themselves of areas they feel drawn to explore.

Updating the Board

Replace Outdated Sections: If they change their mind about something, they can swap it out. This keeps the board true to their latest passions.

Write Notes: They can attach small sticky notes with ideas or steps related to each image.

Immersive Role-Playing Games

If they enjoy imagination, they might like role-playing games (tabletop or simple ones with friends):

Story-Building: Sagittarius can help create the storyline because of their broad thinking and flair for interesting details.

Cooperative Play: Games where players work together toward a shared goal, which suits a Sagittarius who likes friendly interaction over heavy competition.

Short Sessions: If they do not want a long, multi-week campaign, they can opt for "one-shot" role-playing scenarios.

Storing Memories

Character Journals: Keeping short notes about each play session can become a fun record to look back on.

Rotating Game Masters: If the group takes turns leading, it keeps the game varied.

Crafts with an Educational Twist

Sometimes, mixing crafts with real-world learning can really excite a Sagittarius:

Build a Solar System Model: Using styrofoam balls and paint, they can construct the planets and place them in order, picking up astronomy tidbits along the way.

DIY Weather Station: Making a simple rain gauge or a homemade barometer can teach them about weather changes.

Terrarium in a Jar: Placing soil, small plants, and maybe a pebble arrangement in a glass jar. They can watch the mini ecosystem.

Documenting Observations

Take Photos at Each Stage: This helps them see how the project evolves.

Share Online: If they enjoy social media, they might post step-by-step pictures, sparking interest from friends who appreciate science-based crafts.

CHAPTER 15: FAMOUS SAGITTARIUSES

Sagittarius is often linked with a confident outlook, active minds, and a love of learning. While each person is unique, some well-known figures born under this sign do seem to show these traits in their work or public image. In this chapter, we will look at different famous Sagittariuses (plural used for clarity). We will consider individuals from various fields—such as music, film, science, or social impact—and see how their personalities or life choices might echo some of the themes connected with this zodiac sign. Our focus is on introducing examples rather than repeating earlier points about standard Sagittarius traits. Also, we will keep our language straightforward, so it's easy to follow.

Why Look at Famous Sagittariuses?

For some people, looking at public figures can provide a window into how certain star sign traits might appear in action. Of course, no one is defined solely by zodiac influences. Still, it can be interesting to see if the bright qualities of Sagittarius—such as openness, energy, and curiosity—pop up in the stories of these individuals.

We will not claim that these people succeeded just because they are Sagittarians, nor will we claim that all Sagittarians show these same accomplishments. Rather, we can notice certain repeated themes: direct communication style, readiness to try fresh directions, or a lighthearted confidence in front of large crowds. By exploring these figures, we might get new insights into how a Sagittarius outlook can merge with personal aims and creativity.

Musicians and Performers

Taylor Swift (Born December 13, 1989)

Taylor Swift is a singer-songwriter whose career took off at a young age. Many fans admire her ability to reinvent her music and artistic style. She moves from country tunes to pop rhythms, showing a willingness to explore fresh approaches. This adaptability lines up with the Sagittarius taste for variety and openness. Also, she writes personal lyrics that share her feelings and thoughts openly, reflecting the frank side of the sign.

She has also been recognized for talking directly to fans through social media, often in a friendly and unguarded tone. This open, honest method of communication might align with the Sagittarius tendency to speak plainly. In interviews, she can be warm and easy to relate to, showing the bright, approachable spirit often linked to Sagittarius.

Nicki Minaj (Born December 8, 1982)

Nicki Minaj is a rapper, singer, and songwriter known for her bold style, colorful outfits, and confident stage presence. Many see her as a pioneer for women in hip-hop. She tends to speak her mind about industry challenges, not afraid to point out unfair treatment or double standards. This straightforward outspokenness can resonate with the Sagittarius trait of honesty and directness.

Beyond her stage persona, she has engaged in a range of collaborations across different genres, from pop to rap, showing a broad interest that aligns with Sagittarius's love of variety. Fans often talk about her playful humor during interviews, which can reflect the upbeat side of the sign.

Britney Spears (Born December 2, 1981)

Britney Spears is a pop icon who rose to fame in her teenage years. Over a long career, she experienced major highs and well-known challenges. Yet, she also demonstrated resilience, a trait many link with Sagittarius hopefulness. Despite obstacles in her personal life, she continued to produce music and connect with fans worldwide.

Her performances often showcased high energy, dancing, and a cheerful presence, consistent with the spirited vibe that can appear among Sagittarians. She has also spoken candidly at times about her life behind the scenes, echoing the idea that a Sagittarius might show sincerity, even if it risks scrutiny.

Film and Television Personalities

Brad Pitt (Born December 18, 1963)

Brad Pitt is an award-winning actor recognized for his roles in many popular films. He has played a wide range of characters, from adventurous roles to serious dramas, suggesting a comfort with exploring different sides of storytelling. Off screen, he has been involved in various charitable efforts, showing a willingness to engage with broader social or humanitarian issues.

This blend of star power and philanthropic interest can reflect the Sagittarius desire to see beyond personal success and take part in something that might help others. Also, in many interviews, Pitt's easy-going charm comes through, which can be linked to the friendly side of the Archer sign.

Scarlett Johansson (Born November 22, 1984)

Scarlett Johansson's birth date often falls on the borderline between Scorpio and Sagittarius, depending on the year's exact timing.

However, many horoscopes list her as a Sagittarius. She is known for roles that span different genres—action, comedy, drama—suggesting a comfort with variety. Critics and fans often remark on her ability to shift easily from one role to another, mirroring the flexible spirit that some Sagittarians hold.

Johansson has also been open about certain aspects of her personal life and opinions, sometimes facing public scrutiny. Yet, her calm but direct approach to interviews can match the straightforward honesty typically associated with Sagittarius.

Jamie Foxx (Born December 13, 1967)

Jamie Foxx is an actor, comedian, and singer with a broad range of talents. He is recognized for comedic roles as well as serious portrayals, such as playing Ray Charles in "Ray," which earned him an Oscar. This adaptability hints at a willingness to explore different artistic paths. In many talk show appearances, Foxx shows a lively sense of humor and direct comedic timing, attributes that might reflect his Sagittarian side.

He also occasionally steps into philanthropic or social causes, using his platform to speak on relevant topics. This mix of entertainment and a degree of advocacy lines up with the Archer's interest in sharing ideas openly.

Writers and Thinkers

Jane Austen (Born December 16, 1775)

Jane Austen was an English novelist known for works like "Pride and Prejudice" and "Sense and Sensibility." Her witty dialogue and sharp observations about social norms set her books apart in the literary world. Though she wrote during a time when women's roles were limited, she introduced strong, clever female characters. This can be seen as fitting the Sagittarius style—breaking norms and being open about thoughts or critiques.

Austen also used humor to expose societal pressures, similar to how a Sagittarius might use wit to address bigger truths. Her writing remains relevant centuries later, pointing to the timeless appeal of honest storytelling that touches on universal social themes.

Mark Twain (Born November 30, 1835)

Mark Twain, another borderline birth date, is often tied to Sagittarius in many zodiac references. As an American writer known for "The Adventures of Tom Sawyer" and "Adventures of Huckleberry Finn," Twain displayed a combination of humor and social commentary. His direct critiques of society, paired with a humorous style, reflect a bluntness that can feel Sagittarius-like.

In public talks and essays, Twain was not afraid to poke fun at authorities or question popular ideas, which can match the archer's liking for honesty and willingness to say things that might be unpopular. His strong comedic sense also lines up well with typical Sagittarian humor.

Political and Social Leaders

Winston Churchill (Born November 30, 1874)

Winston Churchill, though some might place him on the cusp, is often listed by zodiac sources as a Sagittarius. He served as the Prime Minister of the United Kingdom during challenging times. Known for rousing speeches, he used memorable words to keep spirits high, especially during World War II. This style of direct and impactful communication can be linked to the Sagittarian gift for speaking plainly yet powerfully.

He also showed a sense of humor in private and public remarks, and his actions suggested confidence even under pressure. While some traits may differ from the typical carefree archetype, his ability to adapt strategies and deliver speeches that touched people's hopes ties in with certain aspects of Sagittarius.

Pope Francis (Born December 17, 1936)

Pope Francis, as the leader of the Roman Catholic Church, offers a unique example of a Sagittarius figure in a religious context. He is recognized for an open, humble approach, often addressing social topics in a straightforward manner. Many note his willingness to meet people outside traditional norms, reflecting a more inclusive viewpoint. This aligns with the Archer's trait of wanting to expand horizons and encourage tolerance.

While a pope's role might not be what we typically imagine for a free-spirited Sagittarius, Pope Francis's readiness to speak openly about urgent global issues, care for the poor, and emphasis on kindness could be seen as an expansion of the sign's moral side.

Scientists and Innovators

Ludwig van Beethoven (Baptized December 17, 1770)

Though Beethoven's exact birth date is not completely confirmed—historians only have a baptism date—he is widely cited as a Sagittarius by many sources. He was a groundbreaking composer, pushing classical music into fresh territory. Beethoven was not afraid to break certain musical traditions, which fits the adventurous nature of the Archer sign.

Known for both passionate expression in his music and a sometimes blunt attitude in personal interactions, he might reflect the strong feelings and direct communication style often noted in Sagittarians.

His willingness to experiment and push beyond the norms changed Western music in long-lasting ways.

Grace Hopper (Born December 9, 1906)

Grace Hopper was a computer scientist and United States Navy rear admiral. She pioneered computer programming in the early days of computing. Known for her direct, practical communication, she popularized the term "debugging" after a dead moth was found in a computer. Her readiness to find solutions and break new ground in an unknown field fits with the Sagittarius spirit of seeking fresh approaches.

Hopper was known for speaking at many events, encouraging the next generation to step into the emerging field of technology. Her quotes often encourage people not to fear making mistakes but to keep exploring new possibilities. This forward-looking viewpoint can match the free-thinking and positive style often linked to Sagittarians.

Sports Figures

Giannis Antetokounmpo (Born December 6, 1994)

Giannis Antetokounmpo, nicknamed the "Greek Freak," is a professional basketball player in the NBA. He is known for his strong work ethic, high energy, and big ambitions on the court. His approach to constant skill-building can mirror the Sagittarius openness to growth and willingness to push boundaries.

Off the court, Giannis has shown direct honesty in interviews, discussing his life experiences and personal drive. He also takes part in charitable efforts, reflecting an interest in giving back. This blend of lively passion and openness resonates with common Sagittarius themes.

Larry Bird (Born December 7, 1956)

Larry Bird is a retired basketball legend recognized for his incredible shooting and competitive spirit. Throughout his career with the Boston Celtics, he showed a calm but confident style. He was known for direct talk, sometimes using clever trash talk, which lines up with the straightforward edge of Sagittarius. He aimed high, yet he also was practical in how he approached teamwork.

Post-retirement, Bird moved into coaching and management roles, still showing the same honesty and directness. Many fans appreciate that he never minced words. This approach might mirror the Archer's typical way of saying things plainly, even if it rubs some folks the wrong way.

Artists and Creative Visionaries

Diego Rivera (Born December 8, 1886)

Diego Rivera was a famous Mexican painter known for large murals depicting social themes, history, and everyday people. His art often displayed an honest look at social injustices and culture, reflecting a willingness to confront real issues. A Sagittarius might be drawn to such open expression of deeper truths.

He traveled widely, painting murals in different countries, which fits with the idea of exploration often linked to Sagittarius. Rivera's direct portrayal of political and social subjects can be seen as a bold expression of the Archer's blunt style, used in a creative and impactful way.

Wassily Kandinsky (Born December 16, 1866)

Kandinsky was a Russian painter credited as a pioneer of abstract art. He broke away from realistic imagery, seeking to paint feelings, moods, and musical concepts in shapes and colors. This was a daring move, as many critics initially did not understand such non-representational art. Yet, he held onto his vision, continuing to explore abstract forms.

This bold step beyond traditional art can mirror the Sagittarian trait of stepping into fresh territory, trusting personal insight over established norms. Kandinsky's writings also contained a philosophical angle, linking color and shape to emotional or spiritual concepts, reflecting the Archer's broad-minded perspective.

Media Personalities and Talk Show Hosts

Samuel L. Jackson (Born December 21, 1948)

Samuel L. Jackson is an actor, but also widely recognized for his outspoken presence in media interviews. Known for roles that convey strength and directness, Jackson's own personal style in interviews or public events can be quite frank. He has delivered lines in many films that highlight a take-charge attitude, something that resonates with the fire sign energy.

He has also spoken openly about social issues, reflecting a willingness to point out inequalities or unfairness. This blunt approach to real-world problems can line up with the Sagittarian tendency to speak out rather than hold back.

Tyra Banks (Born December 4, 1973)

Tyra Banks is a television personality, producer, and entrepreneur. She found fame as a model, then expanded into hosting and producing shows like "America's Next Top Model." Her interest in branching out into different roles—modeling, hosting, business, writing—aligns with the Archer's desire for variety.

Tyra Banks is also known for encouraging authenticity and direct feedback on her shows, where she did not hesitate to give strong advice or commentary to contestants. This can connect to the Sagittarian habit of being outspoken while aiming to guide or motivate others.

Patterns and Observations

When we look at these individuals, a few shared themes show up that align with common Sagittarius descriptions:

Adaptability and Range: Many of these figures excel in more than one area or style, from crossing musical genres to branching into new professions.

Direct Communication: Whether it is a comedic style, bold speech, or honest lyrics, the Sagittarian bent toward candor often shines.

Energy and Confidence: Even those in calmer roles display a certain conviction or spark that can be associated with the Archer's fire element.

Desire for Growth and Variety: Many have switched mediums, tried multiple creative paths, or reinvented themselves over time, which fits the restless curiosity attributed to Sagittarius.

Of course, not all Sagittarians in the spotlight show these traits in the same way, and other zodiac signs might share some of these qualities too. Still, noticing these parallels can be entertaining and revealing for those curious about how star sign patterns might appear in real life.

Lessons from Famous Sagittariuses

For people who see themselves in the Archer sign or simply appreciate these examples, there are some takeaways:

Embrace Variety: Many of these figures demonstrate that exploring new avenues or styles can lead to fresh success or satisfaction.

Speak Honestly (With Care): While many Sagittarians are known for frankness, it can be refined into thoughtful honesty that inspires others without causing needless conflict.

Stay Open to Growth: Shifting career paths or artistic directions can be an opportunity, not a setback. It's okay to try new things.

Balance Boldness with Responsibility: These individuals often hold positions of influence. Using that influence wisely shows how a Sagittarian's natural confidence can blend with concern for others.

Avoiding One-Note Stereotypes

It is crucial to remember that not every Sagittarius celebrity matches every single trait of the sign. Real people are complex. Birth charts involve much more than the Sun sign, such as rising signs, Moon signs, and other planetary placements. Also, personal experiences, culture, and environment significantly shape who a person becomes.

Hence, while the examples above might show classic Archer traits—like optimism, directness, or curiosity—these are not exclusive to Sagittarius folks. Observing them simply gives a glimpse into how those qualities might manifest in a public figure's life or career.

Historical and Modern Figures

We have mentioned some older names (like Jane Austen or Beethoven) and more recent ones (like Taylor Swift or Giannis Antetokounmpo). This mix helps show how the sign's potential influences might appear across different centuries and areas of life. Whether it's in sports, literature, music, or activism, the desire to share ideas and push boundaries seems to repeat.

Some Sagittarians might go about it with a cheerful style, like comedic actors or variety show hosts. Others may do so in a quiet but persistent way, as seen in certain artists or innovators. But the unifying thread is often a readiness to test fresh concepts and share them with the world.

Cultural Context and Sagittarius Expression

The way these personalities show Sagittarian traits can also depend on their cultural background. For example, an actor in Hollywood might reveal the sign's traits through flashy interviews and social media updates. An author in a historical setting, like Jane Austen, might channel that same frankness into witty, insightful novels, given the constraints of her time.

This adaptability across different cultures and periods matches the Archer's sense of exploration and flexibility. Sagittarians might find new routes to express energy and clarity, fitting it to the time and place in which they live.

How Their Stories Inspire Others

Fans or admirers of these public figures might feel motivated by how these Sagittarians approach creativity, adversity, or personal growth. For instance:

- **A young musician** might see Taylor Swift's shift from one musical style to another and realize it is okay to explore multiple genres.

- **An aspiring entrepreneur** might look at Tyra Banks's move from modeling to producing and hosting, feeling reassured that it's possible to branch out beyond a single career path.

- **Someone with an interest in writing** might read Mark Twain or Jane Austen and decide to speak their mind with humor and insight.

Each story can offer a nudge toward trying bold ideas or being honest about personal viewpoints. Of course, we must not copy them blindly, but we can absorb bits of encouragement to shape our own paths.

Common Threads with Sagittarius Traits

To sum up the typical themes we see in these well-known Sagittarians:

Honesty and Directness: Many are recognized for speaking in a way that feels genuine, sometimes shocking or funny.

Love of Variety: Their careers and personal pursuits often jump between genres, fields, or styles.

Public Engagement: They often enjoy connecting with a broad audience, whether it is fans, readers, or viewers.

Openness to Reinvention: Reinventing themselves or their craft is less scary to them than it might be to more cautious signs.

Global View or Curiosity: Some show an interest in cultures, traveling, or new intellectual concepts, aligning with the Archer's broad-minded nature.

Potential Pitfalls Observed

Even among the famous, we can see some pitfalls linked to typical Sagittarius patterns:

Overcommitting or Burnout: Some celebrities push themselves too hard or shift directions so often that they find it tough to settle on a stable path.

Too Blunt in Public: A few have faced controversy or misunderstandings due to overly direct remarks, which can happen if the Sagittarian habit of honesty clashes with more sensitive environments.

Struggles with Personal Boundaries: Because they crave space and freedom, being in the public eye can feel restricting or stressful. Some have faced personal crises possibly tied to feeling caged by fame.

These concerns are not unique to Sagittarius, but they can be amplified if the person already leans toward restlessness and open expression.

Looking Forward: Emerging Sagittarius Figures

Each generation brings fresh faces into the limelight. Younger Sagittarians might be rising in areas like digital content creation, online communities, or new music scenes. We might soon see more star sign influences in how they speak to fans on social platforms or develop brand-new forms of entertainment.

In a digital age, Sagittarians may be especially quick to adapt. The sign's inclination to experiment can blend well with fast-changing online trends. Whether launching channels on video platforms or shaping start-ups, we can expect to see new faces that reflect the Archer's spark in these emerging domains.

Learning from a Wide Range of Examples

A key takeaway is that Sagittarius influences can pop up anywhere. We might find them in local activists, lesser-known authors, or community leaders who share these traits but do not have global fame. Recognizing the well-known cases is simply one way to see the sign's outline more clearly. By staying alert, we might spot the same upbeat, direct, open traits in friends, family, or local mentors too.

Suggestions for Aspiring Sagittarius Creators

If you are a Sagittarius wanting to pursue a creative or public path, here are a few practical pointers drawn from the stories of these famous individuals:

Embrace Openness but Plan Enough: While spontaneity is fun, a little structure can help you reach long-term goals.

Use Honesty Wisely: Speak your mind but remember that tone matters. Aim to inspire or clarify rather than offend.

Adapt and Reinvent: If you get stuck, it is okay to shift gears or explore new methods, as many of these figures did.

Stay Grounded: Even if you love big ideas, keep some connection to daily tasks or responsibilities so you do not overextend yourself.

Support Others: Whether it is fans, co-workers, or charities, directing your energy toward helping can bring extra meaning to your endeavors.

Distinguishing Myth from Reality

It is easy to see these famous Sagittariuses as perfect success stories. In truth, each faced personal hardships, failures, and moments of doubt. For instance, some had times when public favor turned against them, or they encountered big personal setbacks. Their ability to persevere might reflect that hopeful spark that many connect with Sagittarius. But it also shows ordinary determination and the help of teams or loved ones.

This highlights the fact that star sign traits alone do not define success or guarantee smooth sailing. Each person's background, network, and personal choices play major roles.

Encouraging Self-Reflection

Reading about these well-known individuals can prompt us to reflect on our own personal style or talents. If you are a Sagittarius, you might spot parallels in your love of variety or direct speech. If you are not a Sagittarius, you can still find inspiration in their stories of creativity or resilience. The main point is to see how certain qualities—openness, optimism, curiosity—can enrich a person's path, no matter their exact birth sign.

Cultural Differences in Recognition

It is worth noting that many of the names listed are from Western popular culture. There are certainly famous Sagittariuses in other regions—actors, musicians, writers, activists—whom we might not commonly hear about in English-speaking media. Each culture has its own style of fame and public life, so it is important to remember that the examples given are only a tiny slice of the full global picture.

For those interested, it can be fun to research popular figures from different cultural backgrounds who also happen to be Sagittarius, comparing how they display the sign's traits in those contexts.

The Ongoing Influence of Their Work

The achievements and expressions of these famous Sagittariuses do not just end when they step away from the stage or screen. Many leave behind songs, books, art, or policy changes that continue to influence future generations. This long-term impact reflects how a spark of creativity or straightforward communication can keep echoing across time.

For instance, Jane Austen's novels remain a staple of English literature classes worldwide. Beethoven's compositions still fill concert halls, centuries after his time. Mark Twain's humor and commentary continue to shape American literature. These examples underline how bold exploration combined with lasting output can carry on well beyond a single lifetime.

CHAPTER 16: COMMON MISUNDERSTANDINGS

Every zodiac sign carries its own reputation, and Sagittarius is no exception. While many see the Archer sign as bright, free-spirited, and open, misunderstandings or oversimplifications can arise. In this chapter, we will talk about the most frequent misconceptions about Sagittarius, explain where these come from, and offer ways to handle or correct them. We will not repeat details from earlier chapters in depth; instead, we will focus on fresh insights into how these misunderstandings appear in daily interactions and how Sagittarians (and those around them) can move past them.

Overview of Why Misunderstandings Happen

A star sign's traits can be broad, and people often reduce them to a handful of basic words, such as "adventurous" or "outspoken." While there may be truth in these words, a single label can become distorted. For example, calling Sagittarius "too blunt" may fail to recognize the care many Archers show in their communication. Similarly, praising them as "fearless explorers" might ignore the anxieties or caution they sometimes feel.

In general, misunderstandings arise when people mix typical sign traits with stereotypes. Some might judge a Sagittarian's free spirit as irresponsibility, or their direct speech as rudeness. Let us see how these misunderstandings appear and how to keep them in perspective.

Misunderstanding #1: "Sagittarians Are Always Wild and Irresponsible"

Where It Comes From
Sagittarius is a fire sign, often linked with high energy and a wish for freedom. This can look like they always want to avoid rules. People might assume Sagittarians are rebellious or run from any responsibility. The sign's symbol, the centaur, half-horse and half-human, may also suggest to some that Sagittarians have uncontrolled impulses like a wild horse.

Reality
While many Sagittarians value personal space and dislike tedious routines, not all are chaotic or immature. Plenty manage to merge spontaneity with steady habits, balancing a love of exploration with real-world duties. They might, for instance, hold a steady job, keep track of bills, and also plan short getaways or creative tasks in spare time. The "wildness" can be more about thinking outside the box or being open to new ideas, not shirking all obligations.

How Sagittarians Can Address It

Show Consistency Where It Counts: By meeting deadlines, paying bills on time, or handling family tasks responsibly, they can counter the idea that they are unreliable.

Explain the Need for Flexibility: If they crave a change in routine, they can clarify that this helps them stay productive and energized, rather than simply running away from tasks.

Set Up Small Structures: A Sagittarius might adopt simple organization methods (like a calendar app) so others see that they can maintain order while still enjoying variety.

Misunderstanding #2: "They Are Too Blunt and Don't Care About Feelings"

Where It Comes From
Sagittarians are known for directness. They often speak plainly, which some interpret as a lack of empathy or a harsh tone. If a Sagittarius person sees a problem, they might say so openly, not realizing how sensitive certain topics can be for others. This leads to the impression that they do not care about others' emotional states.

Reality
Not all Sagittarians are oblivious to others' feelings. Many truly care about loved ones and want to help by giving honest feedback. The sign's trait is typically about sincerity rather than cruelty. They might think being open is a sign of respect, while others might find it uncomfortable if the words land too hard or at the wrong time.

How Sagittarians Can Address It

Assess the Moment: Before offering an opinion, they can check if the other person is ready for frank talk. A quick, "Can I share my honest thoughts?" helps.

Use Gentle Phrasing: Simple additions like "I noticed something that might help you," can reduce the sting of direct statements.

Apologize Sincerely if Needed: If they realize they hurt someone's feelings, acknowledging it shows they do care.

Misunderstanding #3: "They Get Bored Too Easily and Quit Everything"

Where It Comes From
Sagittarians often have many interests, moving from one idea to the next. Outsiders might see them drop hobbies or jobs they once

praised. Friends might assume Sagittarians can never stick with anything and will always move on to the next distraction.

Reality
Yes, Sagittarians like fresh experiences. But many do complete major tasks—such as finishing a degree, building a business, or maintaining a relationship—when they feel genuinely inspired. It's not that they cannot commit; they simply need to see ongoing growth or meaning in what they do. If a project turns repetitive or feels stuck, they may move on to maintain their mental spark.

How Sagittarians Can Address It

Pick Priority Projects: They can choose a few key activities to focus on and see them through to a tangible outcome.

Inject Variety in Long-Term Commitments: Rather than dropping a stable job, they might request new responsibilities or try different approaches.

Communicate Reasons: If they do switch directions, explaining why can show it's not random boredom. For example, "I'm changing roles because I want to learn a new skill," rather than just leaving others guessing.

Misunderstanding #4: "They Are All Big Talk and No Depth"

Where It Comes From
Sagittarius is sometimes viewed as a sign that loves "fun chat," jokes, or casual banter, but does not go deeper. People might think the Archer is only about a surface-level good time, lacking emotional or intellectual seriousness.

Reality

In fact, many Sagittarians enjoy exploring philosophical ideas, personal beliefs, and deeper questions about life. They may love a lively debate or random facts, but that does not mean they cannot handle serious subjects. Some do keep a bright face even when sad, which might cause others to think they do not feel things deeply.

How Sagittarians Can Address It

Engage in Meaningful Discussions: They can show interest in friends' personal dilemmas or deeper world issues, asking thoughtful questions.

Reveal Personal Thoughts: While keeping boundaries, they might share some of their hopes or worries, letting others see a more reflective side.

Balance Humor with Substance: Lightheartedness is great, but mixing in some calm sincerity when the time is right signals genuine depth.

Misunderstanding #5: "They Only Care About Their Own Space and Freedom"

Where It Comes From

Because Sagittarians often insist on personal freedom—such as the ability to choose their schedule or try new things—others may assume they do not want to connect closely or help with group responsibilities. Some interpret this independence as coldness or lack of commitment to family or friends.

Reality

Many Sagittarians do love their independence, but that doesn't mean they cannot be warm, supportive, or devoted to loved ones. They just need to know they are not locked in a situation without options. It is possible for them to build close bonds while still having room to pursue personal interests.

How Sagittarians Can Address It

Offer Help Proactively: By showing up for group tasks, family events, or friend emergencies, they can prove they care.

Clarify Boundaries: If they need alone time, they can explain it's about recharging or thinking, not about pushing people away.

Plan Quality Time: Scheduling fun or meaningful moments with loved ones demonstrates real connection, balancing independence with closeness.

Misunderstanding #6: "They Are Always Happy-Go-Lucky and Don't Understand Sadness"

Where It Comes From

Sagittarius is sometimes described as "the eternal optimist." Folks often assume the Archer never feels down or that they find easy solutions to every problem. This can lead others to think a Sagittarius cannot empathize with darker moods or serious struggles.

Reality

While they lean toward hope, Sagittarians still face worries, sadness, or anxiety like anyone else. Some might hide these heavier emotions to keep their bright image. Others may try to solve issues quickly, but that does not mean they are unaffected by them. They can experience low moods, especially if they feel stuck or restricted in some aspect of life.

How Sagittarians Can Address It

Be Honest When Down: Let close friends or family know if they are having a rough time, rather than masking it.

Listen More: Practicing empathy when others share problems shows they do get it, even if they prefer a hopeful angle.

Offer Balanced Support: Instead of only saying "Cheer up," they can affirm feelings: "I hear you. This is tough. Let's see how we can help each other."

Misunderstanding #7: "They Talk Big But Don't Always Follow Through"

Where It Comes From
Sagittarians might share big ideas in a burst of enthusiasm, but sometimes circumstances change, or they realize their plan was not realistic. When they switch, it can look like they are all hype, without results.

Reality
Sagittarians do get excited about possibilities and might speak about them openly. Not every idea leads to a final product, but that does not mean they never follow through on anything. Often, they filter out which ones matter the most over time. They can see brainstorming as an important part of exploring. Others may interpret it as empty promises.

How Sagittarians Can Address It

Aim for Clarity: They can label early thoughts as "brainstorming" or "just thinking out loud," so people do not expect final action on every idea.

Set a Feasible Timeline: If they do plan to tackle a project, picking a small deadline or step can prove they are serious.

Track Progress: Using a simple planner to show partial completion or updates helps reassure others that they are moving forward.

Misunderstanding #8: "They Can't Handle Deep Emotional Ties"

Where It Comes From
Because of the Archer's need for space, some believe Sagittarians avoid serious emotional bonds like committed relationships, close friendships, or tight family ties. They think Sagittarians flee at the first sign of emotional closeness.

Reality
Sagittarians can value heartfelt relationships. They just approach them differently. They might prefer a partner who supports their independence and meets them halfway on new endeavors. Or they might remain single longer until they find someone who respects their open outlook. Emotional connections can thrive if both sides understand that some personal freedom does not mean a lack of love.

How Sagittarians Can Address It

Discuss Expectations Early: With partners or friends, they can clarify that they care deeply but also need personal breathing room.

Prove Dedication in Actions: By consistently being there in moments of need, they show they can handle closeness.

Balance Independence and Together Time: Planning shared experiences, then allowing each person solo activities, can create harmony.

Misunderstanding #9: "They Are Reckless Daredevils Without Fear"

Where It Comes From
Stories and images of the centaur with a bow might lead people to see Sagittarians as unstoppable risk-takers. Some do enjoy physical adventures—hiking in unknown places, spontaneous sports—but that does not always mean they never feel concern or plan ahead.

Reality
Sagittarians often weigh the possible rewards of taking a bold step. They may be more comfortable with risk than some signs, but that does not mean they blindly dive into danger. They can feel fear or caution, especially if the risk might harm others or jeopardize important goals. However, they might handle it with humor or a positive spin, leading observers to think they are fearless.

How Sagittarians Can Address It

Share Thought Process: If they plan an adventurous activity, letting friends know they have considered safety steps counters the reckless label.

Acknowledge Nerves: Admitting when they are nervous shows they are not just ignoring the risks.

Encourage Others to Prepare: They can demonstrate they do plan properly, urging group members to bring the right gear or understand the route, for example.

Why These Misconceptions Persist

Zodiac clichés, personal anecdotes, and oversimplified horoscopes in popular media keep these ideas going. Also, some Sagittarians do exhibit these traits in an exaggerated way, which can reinforce stereotypes. If a person meets just one Archer who is overly blunt or scatterbrained, they might generalize that all Sagittarians are the same.

Additionally, the sign's positive reputation for optimism can overshadow deeper aspects, causing others to assume Sagittarians cannot be serious. Once a label sticks, it can be hard to shake.

How Sagittarians Can Move Past Stereotypes

Practice Self-Awareness: Regularly check in on how they communicate and handle tasks to see if they are reinforcing a negative view or if they are misunderstood.

Explain Motivations: If someone complains they are unreliable, the Sagittarius can clarify that they simply changed direction due to new info or better options, not laziness.

Show Vulnerability: By letting close friends or relatives see moments of doubt or sadness, they counter the "always happy" misconception.

Listen to Feedback: If multiple people mention the same concern, it might be worth adjusting. A small tweak, like a kinder tone or a bit more planning, can go a long way.

How Others Can Better Understand Sagittarius

Ask Questions: Instead of assuming a Sagittarius is bored, ask them why they are shifting. They might have a valid reason.

Appreciate Candor: Recognize that honesty is meant to be helpful, not hurtful. Politely letting them know if a comment was too sharp can improve the conversation.

Give Them Space: Understand that occasional solo time or freedom to experiment is part of their nature, not a personal snub.

Encourage Their Best Traits: If you see them excited about a project, offer assistance or share resources. They thrive on supportive positivity.

Misconceptions in the Workplace

In a professional environment, people might label a Sagittarius coworker as "unreliable" or "unpredictable" just because they propose new approaches. Or a blunt email from them might be misread as rude. Colleagues can think the Sagittarius does not care about rules or meeting times. Here are ways to address that:

Be Transparent About Work Style: A Sagittarius can say, "I like bringing fresh ideas, but I also respect our processes. Let me know if I overstep."

Use Scheduling Tools: Even if they prefer flexibility, using calendar reminders or to-do apps helps show they can be counted on.

Offer Constructive Feedback: If a coworker finds their directness jarring, they can request input: "Let me know if my tone seems off so I can adjust."

Relationships and Dating Misunderstandings

Partners might assume a Sagittarius is not serious about the relationship if they say things like, "I want to travel alone for a week" or "I need space." In reality, that might just be how they balance closeness with personal exploration. Another common issue is the Archer's directness. They might point out a partner's flaw quickly, intending to help, but the partner interprets it as cold critique.

Clear Communication About Needs: Explaining that solitude occasionally helps them recharge can reassure the partner it is not about running away.

Gentle Delivery of Criticism: Even if the feedback is valid, choosing kind words keeps the bond strong.

Shared Adventures: Suggesting joint trips or projects can show the partner they value togetherness, not just independence.

Family Ties and Sagittarius Myths

Family members might typecast the Sagittarius child or sibling as "the restless one who never stays in one place." If the family is more traditional, they might think the Archer avoids basic chores or stable jobs. Over time, this can create tension.

Explain Personal Goals: Telling parents or siblings about specific objectives helps them see there is a plan behind the apparent wandering.

Fulfill Core Family Duties: Taking responsibility for certain tasks and finishing them can counter the idea that they are always on the run.

Plan Occasional Gatherings: Initiating family get-togethers shows they do care about staying connected.

Social Circles and Friendships

Friends might label a Sagittarius as "the friend who always changes plans at the last minute." While sometimes this is true if they spot a more interesting event, many Sagittarians do value their friendships. They just might not like feeling locked into an event too far in advance.

Honesty Up Front: If they are unsure they can attend, it is better to say "I'll try, but I might have another commitment" rather than giving a firm yes and then bailing.

Propose Alternatives: If they skip a group outing, they can suggest a different time or place to hang out. This shows effort in maintaining the connection.

Keep Communication Open: Sending a quick message if plans must change can prevent friends from feeling stood up.

Handling Cross-Cultural Misunderstandings

Different cultures have unique norms about communication. A Sagittarius traveling or living in a new region might unintentionally cross lines if direct talk is considered rude there. Or they may be seen as aloof if they do not conform to local social routines.

Observe Local Customs: Noticing how people greet, share opinions, or handle time can help a Sagittarius adapt their style.

Learn Polite Phrases in That Culture: Even if they do not speak the language fluently, showing respect through basic courtesy terms fosters better connections.

Explain Their Style Gently: If they plan to be very open, they can mention, "I tend to speak directly. Please let me know if I say something in a way that seems impolite."

Internet and Social Media Misconceptions

Online spaces can amplify misunderstandings. A Sagittarian might tweet blunt opinions or rapidly switch topics, leaving followers confused. Some might call them "inconsistent" or "too vocal" on social platforms.

Use Tone Indicators or Emojis: This can soften direct remarks, helping others see they are not meant as harsh.

Segment Topics: If they have multiple interests, organizing them by separate accounts or hashtags can show they are not just jumping aimlessly but exploring varied themes in an organized way.

Engage Kindly in Debates: Being direct is fine, but insults or overly aggressive language can feed negative labels. Polite but firm expressions help keep online debates constructive.

Celebrity Culture and Star Sign Rumors

Sometimes, famous Sagittarians might do something controversial, and fans paint all Sagittarians as a certain way. For instance, if a popular singer known for being a Sagittarius abruptly cancels a show, people might say, "See, Sagittarians are unreliable." These sweeping judgments can stick.

- **Recognize Individual Factors:** That singer's decision might have health or contract reasons, not just a star sign trait.

- **Separate Personal Choice from Zodiac:** A single example does not define the sign as a whole, and fans should be aware that many variables influence a celebrity's actions.

- **Stay Balanced:** Observing patterns can be fun, but extreme claims about every Sagittarius because of one public figure's behavior can lead to misguided stereotypes.

The Role of Humor in Addressing Misunderstandings

Sagittarians often use humor naturally. This can be a tool to defuse tension around stereotypes. For example, if someone says, "You Sagittarians never finish anything," a Sagittarius might reply with a lighthearted line like, "I finished dinner last night, so that's progress!" This approach can reduce defensiveness, while still allowing for clarity.

Humor, though, should not dismiss genuine concerns. If the misunderstanding is severe—like repeated conflicts at work—more direct conversation is needed. But for mild misconceptions, playful replies can show that while they understand the stereotype, they refuse to be boxed in by it.

When Sagittarians Do Match the Negative Traits

Sometimes, a particular Sagittarius might indeed be irresponsible, extremely blunt, or always bored. Not all negative stereotypes are baseless for every individual. In these cases, a person can grow by acknowledging that the trait might be hurting their relationships or career.

- **Self-Reflection:** They can ask themselves if they truly want to improve or if they see value in changing.

- **Gradual Adjustments:** Big transformations rarely happen overnight. Trying small steps—like committing to one project fully—can build better habits.

- **Seek Accountability:** If they struggle with follow-through, a friend or mentor can remind them of their goals, ensuring they do not drift too far.

Breaking the Cycle of Oversimplified Labels

Over time, constant repetition of, "You're such a typical Sagittarius," in a negative sense can shape a person's identity. They might start acting out those stereotypes or feeling defensive. Breaking this cycle requires both the individual Sagittarian and those around them to remember that a person's character is more than a few zodiac words.

Focus on the Person, Not Just the Sign: Loved ones can appreciate the unique mix of personality traits, experiences, and talents, rather than using only "Sagittarius" as an explanation.

Celebrate Strengths: Notice the positive outcomes of the sign's open-mindedness or optimism. Recognizing good qualities can balance any negative assumptions.

Respect Individual Journeys: Each person grows at their own pace. The sign alone does not set a final personality blueprint.

Looking Beyond the Sun Sign

Many of these misunderstandings arise from focusing only on a person's Sun sign. In-depth astrology considers the Moon, rising sign, and more. A Sagittarius with a more grounded rising sign might not appear restless, or a Sagittarius with a gentle Moon sign could come off as extremely empathetic. Recognizing these layers can reduce the chance of painting every Archer with the same brush.

For those who do not follow astrology deeply, it still helps to remember that personality is shaped by family background, personal experiences, culture, and personal choices—far beyond any zodiac classification.

CHAPTER 17: HANDLING CONFLICT

Sagittarius is often linked with optimism, direct speech, and openness. Yet, like anyone else, Sagittarians face conflicts in everyday life—whether at home, with friends, at work, or even within themselves. While they have a bright outlook, disagreements can still arise. Handling those disputes effectively requires understanding certain typical Sagittarius responses, as well as learning methods to calm heated situations. This chapter will explore how Sagittarians might respond to conflict, why certain habits can cause friction, and practical ways to handle disagreements peacefully. We will avoid repeating large ideas from previous chapters, focusing on new angles: how the Sagittarius style influences conflict dynamics, how they can keep respect and fairness in tough moments, and how they can harness their hopeful energy to reach better solutions.

Why Conflict Happens

Conflict is a normal part of human relationships. It can appear whenever two people have different goals, expectations, or communication styles. For Sagittarius, conflicts might emerge if:

Direct Speech Hurts Feelings: A Sagittarian who believes in honest talk might unknowingly upset someone more sensitive.

Need for Freedom Collides with Rules: If a family member, romantic partner, or boss imposes strict guidelines, a Sagittarius can feel cornered or annoyed, leading to arguments.

Impulsive Reactions: In tense situations, the Sagittarius might blurt out a thought without pausing, sparking bigger disagreements than needed.

Even with the best intentions, conflicts occur. But they do not have to become damaging if approached with thoughtfulness and fairness.

Sagittarius Traits That Affect Conflict

Before diving into strategies, let's pinpoint which Sagittarius qualities might intensify or defuse conflict:

Openness and Candor: This can be helpful because honest talk can resolve misunderstandings quickly. However, if the candor is too sharp, it might provoke defensiveness in others.

Optimism and Hope: Many Sagittarians believe problems can be fixed, which gives them the motivation to try solutions. On the other hand, if they brush off serious concerns with too much positivity, they might frustrate people who want deeper discussion.

Restlessness Under Stress: During a fight, a Sagittarius might prefer to walk away or do something else, rather than stay calm and work through it. This can leave issues unresolved.

Flexible Mind: Sagittarians often adapt quickly, which can be an advantage when looking for compromises. But if they switch positions too abruptly, others may feel the conversation is unsteady.

Understanding these tendencies helps the Archer be aware of which habits to watch in a heated moment, turning conflict from a destructive clash into a learning experience.

Common Conflict Triggers for Sagittarius

Though conflicts vary by person, certain themes can pop up repeatedly for Sagittarians:

Feeling Trapped or Controlled: If a partner, boss, or friend tries to micromanage, the Sagittarius might respond with irritation or open defiance.

Being Criticized Unfairly: Sagittarians are not afraid of feedback, but if it seems harsh or illogical, they might snap back or become defensive.

Promises They Could Not Keep: Sometimes, a Sagittarius overestimates what they can do. When they cannot deliver, frustration flares on both sides.

Misinformed Opinions or Half-Truths: They value honesty, so if they sense someone is hiding something or spreading untrue statements, they might confront the issue directly, risking a heated exchange.

Recognizing these triggers ahead of time lets them step back when they spot trouble coming. A little forethought can stop minor tensions from exploding into bigger disputes.

Approaches That Can Escalate Conflict

Sometimes, the Sagittarius style might accidentally fan the flames rather than calm them. Here are risky approaches:

Sarcasm as a Shield: While humor can be disarming, sarcastic jokes in the midst of an argument might worsen matters if the other person feels mocked.

Storming Off: An impulsive exit might seem like an escape, but it can leave the other party feeling unheard or abandoned.

Overriding the Other Person's Feelings: A Sagittarius might say, "It's not a big deal," but if the other person is clearly upset, that response can feel dismissive.

Turning Everything Into a Philosophical Debate: While the Archer loves big ideas, sometimes the other person wants practical solutions or emotional support. Overly broad discussions can sideline the real issue.

Avoiding these tactics is not about ignoring the Sagittarius nature but rather tempering it with empathy and patience. By staying mindful, they can keep arguments constructive.

Productive Strategies for Handling Conflict

Use the "Pause" Method: When emotions run high, a quick pause allows the Sagittarius to gather thoughts. They might say, "Let me think for a moment," which signals they are not ignoring the problem but trying to respond fairly.

Adopt "I" Statements: Instead of pointing fingers with "You always do this," a Sagittarius can say, "I feel upset when this happens." This shift in language lessens the chance of the other person feeling personally attacked.

Offer Solutions, Not Just Critique: If they spot a problem, they can also propose a helpful fix. For instance, "I think we need clearer guidelines on who does which task," rather than just "You never do your share."

Ask for the Other Person's View: A Sagittarian might easily jump to their own arguments. But pausing to say, "How do you see this situation?" can show willingness to understand, cooling the temperature of the dispute.

Close with Constructive Steps: After talking, summing up next steps ensures clarity. For example, "So, we agree to divide tasks in a new way, and we'll check back in a week." This helps avoid lingering confusion.

Such strategies channel the Archer's directness into measured communication. Honesty still thrives, but it is cushioned by courtesy and practical outcomes.

Conflict with Friends or Siblings

In friendships and sibling relationships, Sagittarians might be the ones who speak up first about an issue. This can be good if done politely, since unspoken resentments cause bigger rifts later. However, they should watch for these pitfalls:

Overstepping Boundaries: Offering direct advice to a sibling or friend who did not ask for it can spark resistance. Even if the suggestion is well-meaning, the other person might prefer to find their own path.

Inconsistent Attention: A Sagittarius can get caught up in new interests, sometimes leaving friends or siblings feeling forgotten. This can lead to accusations of "You don't care."

Lightening the Mood Too Soon: If a serious matter is on the table—like finances or health concerns—a Sagittarius joke might land badly. Some conflicts require acknowledging the gravity before moving on.

Helpful Approaches

Ask Permission to Give Input: "I have a thought on that. Do you want my honest opinion?" This shows respect for the friend's or sibling's space.

Schedule a Direct Talk: Setting aside time to address big issues calmly can prevent them from creeping up in random moments.

Use Humor Gently: Humor can still help, but time it properly. After the issue is partly resolved, a light laugh can relieve tension, not overshadow it.

Conflict with Parents or Authority Figures

Sagittarians who dislike rigid control can struggle with parents, teachers, or bosses who impose firm rules. The clash arises when the Archer feels stifled, while the authority figure sees them as resistant or disobedient. In these moments:

Listen to Their Reasoning: Even if the rule feels pointless, hearing out the authority's explanation might reveal concerns about safety or fairness. This can help the Sagittarius propose an alternative that still meets the bigger goal.

Suggest Middle Ground: A Sagittarian can say, "I understand we need structure. What if I handle these tasks in my own style, as long as I meet the deadline?" This approach respects the rule while preserving some freedom.

Stay Polite but Firm: Instead of a heated outburst, calmly restating their viewpoint can show maturity: "I see your worries, but I also believe I can do well if I have a bit more flexibility."

When authority figures feel respected, they are more likely to return that respect, leading to workable compromises. Sagittarians excel when they realize that a bit of courtesy often gets them more leeway, not less.

Conflict in Romantic Relationships

Because Sagittarians crave both closeness and independence, romantic partners might feel confused about boundaries. Conflicts here can revolve around:

Jealousy or Feeling Neglected: If a partner interprets the Sagittarius's need for personal time as rejection, tensions brew.

Disagreement on Future Plans: The Sagittarius might yearn for open-ended possibilities, while the partner may want a set plan for careers, living arrangements, or family.

Overly Blunt Critiques: Telling a partner, "You're overreacting," or "That's silly," can wound feelings deeply.

Constructive Relationship Tips

Clarify Space Requirements: Let the partner know exactly how much alone time is needed, and reassure them it does not reduce love or commitment.

Find Shared Goals: They can propose, "We can plan short-term while leaving some room for changes. Let's agree on the next six months, then see how we feel."

Listen to Emotional Cues: If the partner is upset, focusing on empathy first—"I hear you're hurting"—is key before offering a quick fix.

Use Soothing Words: Rather than, "You're overreacting," try, "I see this is important to you. Let's unpack why it feels so intense."

A healthy romantic bond for a Sagittarius relies on mutual respect for each other's needs, balanced with open communication that remains gentle despite the Archer's directness.

Workplace Conflicts

At work, Sagittarians might clash with coworkers or supervisors if:

Projects Lack Excitement: The Archer could grow impatient with boring tasks. If they slack off, others might feel they are not pulling their weight.

Team Members Fear Their Candid Remarks: A blunt comment in a meeting can cause friction, especially if the team is used to a polite, indirect style.

Deadlines Are Missed Due to Distraction: If a Sagittarius juggles too many ideas, they might overlook a crucial deadline, annoying colleagues who depend on them.

Strategies to Prevent Work Conflicts

Focus on Team Goals: Even if the task seems dull, the Sagittarius can remind themselves of the bigger picture—completing the project helps the group, leading to new possibilities.

Offer Constructive Input in Meetings: Instead of just pointing out flaws, they can phrase feedback like, "I notice a challenge here—maybe we can address it by doing X."

Track Commitments: Using a shared calendar or reminder apps helps them avoid forgetting tasks. Clear updates to coworkers or the boss about their progress also reduce misunderstandings.

If disputes arise, they can resolve them by showing they respect team processes while still contributing fresh ideas. The Archer's positivity can be a major plus, but it needs to be backed up by follow-through.

Emotional Self-Conflict

Conflicts are not always external. A Sagittarius might battle with themselves internally over choices, goals, or regrets. They may feel torn between the desire for adventure and the need for stability, or they might question whether they are being too impulsive. Such internal tension can manifest in stress, mood swings, or feeling trapped.

Ways to Address Inner Conflict

Structured Self-Reflection: Setting aside time to write down pros and cons of a decision. This clarifies what they truly want instead of jumping between extremes.

Seeking Advice from a Trusted Person: A mentor or close friend might offer a perspective that balances freedom and responsibility.

Breaking Down Goals: If they feel stuck, dividing larger aims into smaller steps helps them see progress. This approach reduces the sense of all-or-nothing.

Allowing Self-Compassion: Understanding that it is okay to change course if the initial path no longer fits. Guilt or shame over not continuing a project can be replaced with an acceptance that new info leads to updated decisions.

Inner conflicts often revolve around the Archer's broad horizon. By giving themselves room to explore in a measured way, they transform self-clashes into personal evolution.

Cooling Down Methods

No matter the type of conflict, emotional heat can rise quickly. Sagittarians sometimes respond with outbursts or attempts at quick humor. Cooling down techniques can help defuse tension before it escalates:

Physical Reset: A short walk, quick stretches, or stepping outside can calm the mind. This is especially helpful if they sense themselves becoming frustrated.

Breathing Exercises: Slowly inhaling for a few counts, holding briefly, and exhaling can lower stress levels, making them less likely to speak rashly.

Mental Reminders: A phrase like, "I want a solution, not a fight," repeated internally, keeps them focused on resolution rather than "winning."

Writing Feelings Down: Jotting a few notes or bullet points can prevent them from blurting out the first harsh phrase that comes to mind.

Listening to the Other Person's Tone: If the other person is also agitated, the Sagittarius might hold back a strong reply to avoid throwing more fuel on the fire.

Once calmer, they can approach the issue from a place of reasoned directness instead of heated reaction.

Long-Term Conflict Resolution

Some conflicts do not end in one talk. A significant disagreement—like a family feud, ongoing workplace tension, or repeated clashes in a relationship—demands ongoing effort. Sagittarians can leverage these steps:

Follow-Up Discussions: Checking back after a few days or weeks ensures that any solution is really working. If not, they can adjust it rather than ignoring new friction.

Clear Agreements in Writing: For bigger disputes, writing down agreed-upon steps can prevent "Did we agree on that?" confusion later. This might feel formal, but it helps keep all sides accountable.

Involving a Neutral Mediator: If conflict is deeply entrenched, a counselor, coach, or trusted mutual friend might help keep the conversation fair.

Reflecting on Patterns: The Sagittarius might notice repeated triggers and aim to change behaviors. For instance, if every conflict starts after they vanish for days without explanation, they can work on consistent communication.

By treating conflict resolution as a process rather than a single event, the Archer can transform friction into improved understanding and trust over time.

Conflict vs. Assertion of Personal Beliefs

Sagittarians love discussing wide-ranging topics. Sometimes, lively debates about politics, religion, or lifestyle choices can seem like conflict, even if it is just strong opinions clashing. The line between healthy debate and outright conflict depends on respect and willingness to hear the other side.

Stay Curious: Instead of stating, "You're wrong," a Sagittarius might say, "That's interesting. Why do you believe that?" This approach fosters a more open exchange.

Avoid Personal Insults: Once name-calling or insinuations start, debate turns into hostility. Sagittarians can channel their directness into addressing ideas rather than attacking the person.

Know When to Stop: If the discussion becomes heated and neither side is listening, it might be wise to pause. They can say, "Let's revisit this when we're both calmer," rather than pushing it to an ugly endpoint.

These guidelines keep lively debates from damaging relationships.

Teaching Children or Younger Folks About Conflict

For a Sagittarius parent, older sibling, or mentor, sharing conflict-handling insights with younger ones can be valuable. Because Sagittarians often lead by example, their actions during a dispute become a model:

Show Calm Reactions: If a child sees them handle a household disagreement calmly, it teaches the child that direct talk does not have to be angry.

Encourage Emotional Vocabulary: Urging kids to say, "I'm upset because…" fosters clarity. The straightforward style of Sagittarius can help children see honesty as normal.

Reward Resolution Efforts: When a younger sibling or child tries to fix a problem or apologize, a Sagittarian adult can acknowledge that effort, reinforcing positive conflict resolution.

This kind of guidance helps the next generation approach differences with courage, clarity, and respect.

Cultural Differences in Conflict Styles

Sagittarians who travel or interact with people from different cultural backgrounds might face confusion if each culture approaches conflict differently. Some cultures prefer indirect hints, while others value direct confrontation. The Archer's blunt talk can clash with more reserved norms, or it might be welcomed in a straightforward environment. To manage this:

Observe Local Customs: Noticing how the locals discuss problems can guide the Sagittarius in softening or adjusting their approach.

Ask Polite Questions: If unsure, they can privately inquire how to handle disagreements in that setting. People often appreciate the sincerity of wanting to respect cultural norms.

Blend Styles: The Sagittarius can keep honesty but wrap it in gentler language, or allow more time for the other side to respond, ensuring they do not appear overly pushy.

This flexibility can turn potential cultural misunderstandings into respectful collaborations.

Conflict and the Online World

Digital conflicts can escalate fast due to misunderstandings of tone or quick emotional reactions. A Sagittarian might dash off a blunt comment on social media, leading to heated exchanges. Or they might feel attacked by others' responses to their direct style. Strategies for online conflict:

Pause Before Sending: A short wait to read over the comment or email can prevent hasty, regrettable statements.

Use Clear, Polite Language: Without facial expressions, the other person might not sense the Archer's playful mood. Words must be chosen carefully.

Take Discussions Offline if Deep: If the debate is important, a voice call or face-to-face talk might be more productive. Text-based fights often loop in circles.

Avoid Public Shaming: Tagging someone in a negative post or airing grievances in front of an audience can multiply tension. Private messages can keep things calmer.

When Sagittarians adapt their honesty to digital etiquette, they can maintain genuine expression without sparking endless online drama.

Apologies and Forgiveness

Sometimes, a Sagittarius might realize they crossed a line—maybe they used too strong a tone or stepped on someone's feelings. Owning up can be powerful:

Direct Apology: They can say, "I'm sorry I spoke harshly. I didn't mean to disrespect you." Simple, clear language that shows genuine remorse is effective.

Avoid Defensiveness: Adding, "But you made me mad," dilutes the apology. Owning one's action fully fosters quicker healing.

Repair Actions: Beyond words, a small follow-up gesture—like helping with a task, offering a kind note, or scheduling time to talk—shows sincerity.

Self-Forgiveness: If they regret how they handled a conflict, they can learn from it without dwelling on shame. This frees them to do better next time.

Apologies from a Sagittarius can carry special weight, given that they are known for honesty. When done thoughtfully, it reaffirms relationships in a positive way.

Building Long-Term Peaceful Habits

Over time, adopting conflict resolution habits can enrich a Sagittarius's relationships and sense of personal well-being. A few long-term practices:

Frequent Check-Ins: They can ask friends or relatives, "How are we feeling about this arrangement?" Doing so prevents unspoken annoyances from boiling over.

Journaling Lessons: After a conflict, writing what worked or didn't can form a personal reference for future arguments.

Mentoring Others in Resolution: If they become skilled, they might help coworkers or younger folks handle disputes, reinforcing their own practice.

Balancing Confrontation with Patience: They do not have to address every small annoyance instantly. Sometimes waiting a little until they have calm perspective yields better outcomes.

These habits reduce the repeated cycle of friction, allowing Sagittarians to keep their relationships and goals running smoothly.

Recognizing When to End a Conflict

Not all conflicts lead to mutual agreement. Sometimes, the healthiest choice is stepping away or agreeing to disagree. For instance, if the other party refuses any compromise or if the argument becomes personal or abusive, continuing might be pointless or harmful.

Set Boundaries: A Sagittarian can say, "I respect your view, but I won't continue this if we can't keep it respectful."

Seek Support: If the conflict is toxic or if the other side is verbally harming them, looking for a neutral mediator or professional guidance can help.

Accept That Not Everyone Aligns: A basic difference in core values might remain. The Archer's open mindset can let them move on without hostility, acknowledging that not all disagreements find resolution.

Deciding when to end a dispute does not mean giving up on direct communication. It means preserving emotional health when resolution is not feasible.

Lessons Learned from Conflict

Handled well, conflict can teach Sagittarians:

Better Listening Skills: Each dispute is a chance to practice hearing someone else's perspective before jumping in.

Empathy and Flexibility: They might find innovative compromises that broaden their viewpoint.

Deeper Self-Insight: Reflecting on why a certain topic triggered them can show hidden fears or desires.

Improved Relationships: Overcoming a tough argument often strengthens bonds if both parties communicate respectfully.

In this sense, conflict is not purely negative. For a sign that loves growth, seeing disagreements as opportunities to learn new interpersonal skills can turn them into a valuable experience. Though they might prefer to avoid tension, the reality is that well-managed disputes can deepen trust and mutual respect.

Turning Conflict into Shared Understanding

When a Sagittarian invests in conflict resolution, the effect can be transformative. Here are steps to harness that potential:

Lead with Warmth: Even if they are upset, beginning with a calm greeting or an acknowledgment of the other person's positive qualities can soften defenses.

Speak from Personal Values: If honesty is key for them, they can say, "I'm being direct because I value truth, but I want to respect your feelings." This clarifies intentions.

Invite Win-Win Ideas: Ask, "How can we fix this so we both feel okay?" People are more open when they see their perspective is included.

Show Gratitude After Resolution: If they reach an agreement, a simple "Thank you for working this out with me" can close the conversation on a friendly note.

A commitment to fairness matches the Sagittarius spirit. They can turn a tense moment into a dialogue that fosters deeper understanding, aligning with their broader outlook on life.

Conflict Scenarios to Practice

To become adept, Sagittarians might role-play scenarios or mentally rehearse how they would handle them:

A Friend Cancels Plans Repeatedly: Instead of angrily accusing them of being inconsiderate, they might calmly ask, "What's going on? Is there a reason you keep canceling?"

A Coworker Critiques Their Work Publicly: Rather than snapping back in front of everyone, the Sagittarius can request a private talk to find out the coworker's concerns.

A Partner Is Upset Over a Minor Issue: If the partner is angry that they forgot a small chore, the Sagittarius might listen fully, acknowledge the frustration, then propose a quick fix or apology.

An Online Stranger Starts a Heated Debate: The Archer can try clarifying questions or politely stepping away if it becomes toxic.

By pre-thinking possible responses, they reduce impulsive reactions that might escalate tensions.

Encouraging Others to Resolve Conflict

Sometimes, Sagittarians see two friends in conflict, or colleagues at odds. Their direct style can help mediate if they handle it carefully:

Create a Safe Space: Offer to host a calm discussion, ensuring each side can speak without interruptions.

Ask Neutral Questions: "What do you feel is the core issue?" or "What would make this better for you?" This shows no bias.

Summarize Common Points: Sagittarians can highlight shared ground—"It sounds like both of you want a good outcome for the team"—which fosters unity.

Suggest a Next Step: Encourage them to decide on a small action to move forward, like a follow-up conversation or an agreed-upon rule.

If done tactfully, a Sagittarian's honesty and optimism can defuse tension among others, turning them into a helpful peacemaker.

Involving Professional Help

There are times when personal or workplace conflicts become too tangled, intense, or longstanding for casual solutions. Therapy, counseling, or mediation can be wise. A Sagittarian might initially resist, fearing it is too formal, but professional guidance can provide:

Structured Communication Tools: Trained mediators can guide the discussion so it remains respectful.

Objective Perspective: A neutral party sees patterns that friends or relatives might miss.

Conflict-Management Skills: The Sagittarian can learn methods for listening, clarifying, and empathizing, which they can apply in future disputes.

Accepting professional help is not a sign of weakness. For a sign that treasures growth, it can be an invaluable resource, especially if the conflict is deep-rooted or repeatedly flares up.

CHAPTER 18: SAGITTARIUS & SELF-IMPROVEMENT

Sagittarians often have a thirst for knowledge, new experiences, and personal growth. While earlier chapters touched on how they learn or explore interests, here we will focus on practical self-improvement—ways that a Sagittarius can build better habits, sharpen talents, or develop personal skills, all while balancing their desire for freedom. We will bring in fresh angles, talking about setting goals, overcoming procrastination, managing mental well-being, and becoming the best version of the Archer without feeling trapped by rigid routines.

What Self-Improvement Means for Sagittarius

Self-improvement can look different depending on the person. For Sagittarius:

Expanding Horizons: The Archer thrives on learning. Improving themselves could mean picking up new languages, reading advanced topics, or training in novel fields.

Finding Balance Between Freedom and Structure: They dislike feeling boxed in, so they might avoid typical self-improvement plans that are overly strict. Instead, they can find flexible systems that allow enough wiggle room.

Aligning Growth with Passions: Many Sagittarians excel when their goals match their personal enthusiasms—like traveling, creative arts, or social interactions.

By customizing self-improvement so it suits their free-spirited style, they are more likely to stick with it and see meaningful results.

Identifying Personal Goals

Before diving into new habits, it helps to pinpoint what the Sagittarius wants to improve. Some might aim to sharpen job skills, others might want better time management, and some might focus on emotional intelligence. Clear goals:

Prevent Aimlessness: Without a target, a Sagittarius might hop from one idea to the next without lasting impact.

Foster Motivation: Seeing a direct purpose helps them stay energized, especially if they can imagine the exciting outcomes.

Allow for Adjustments: They can pick short-term goals (like learning basic guitar chords) and long-term ones (like mastering advanced songs), leaving room to adapt if their interests shift.

It is important not to overstuff the list. A few well-chosen aims can keep them engaged without overwhelming their sense of freedom.

The Challenge of Routine for Sagittarius

One key obstacle is that many self-improvement paths involve consistent practice or daily repetition. A Sagittarius might balk at strict timetables, quickly becoming restless. However, routine can be approached in a more dynamic way:

Modular Scheduling: Instead of "Every day at 6 AM, I do X," they might set a weekly total, such as "I will work out three times this week, on whichever days feel right."

Variety within Consistency: If they want to improve physical fitness, they might rotate swimming, running, and dancing, rather than repeating the same activity.

Short Bursts: Using 15- to 20-minute focused sessions can prevent boredom. This might be reading for 20 minutes about coding or painting quickly, then switching tasks if needed.

Adopting flexible structures allows them to stay on track without feeling shackled by the same process day in and day out.

Overcoming Procrastination and Distraction

Because Sagittarius craves fresh input, they can lose interest in tasks once the novelty wears off. This can sabotage self-improvement if they keep jumping to new endeavors. Possible solutions:

Micro-Commitments: Promise to do a small part of the task each day (like writing 100 words or practicing 10 minutes of an instrument). Once started, they might continue longer if they feel good momentum.

Public Accountability: Telling friends or posting a mild update can push them to keep going, because they do not want to appear flaky.

Gamification: Turning progress into a simple point system or leveling up approach can inject fun. For instance, awarding themselves a "star" each time they complete a study session.

Tracking Small Wins: Keeping a note of daily achievements—like "Wrote a paragraph," "Learned a new chord," or "Read 10 pages"—shows them they are advancing, even if slowly.

Such methods ensure they do not abandon goals at the first hint of routine fatigue.

Building Discipline Without Feeling Restricted

Sagittarians might fear that discipline equals losing freedom. Yet discipline can be seen as the ability to do what benefits them in the long run, not forced compliance. To reframe discipline:

Empowerment, Not Constraint: Realizing that consistent effort leads to mastery, which increases freedom and options later, can motivate them to put in the work now.

Self-Chosen Boundaries: If the Archer sets their own guidelines, it feels less like external control. For example, deciding "I'll only check social media after I finish this hour of study" is a self-imposed rule.

Reward-based Milestones: They can attach small fun rewards—like trying a new café or watching a favorite show—after completing a self-improvement milestone. This keeps the process exciting.

By seeing discipline as a bridge to bigger adventures, they reduce the sense of being "tied down."

Mentoring and Learning from Others

Sagittarians appreciate shared knowledge and might boost self-improvement by seeking mentors or joining groups:

Study Groups: Whether it is a writing club, language exchange, or skill-sharing circle, being around others fosters motivation. People can exchange tips, encouraging the Archer to remain engaged.

Online Communities: Virtual forums and video chats can help them connect with teachers or peers worldwide, appealing to their global interest.

Listening to Experts: Tuning into podcasts or watching interviews with accomplished folks in their area of interest can stir inspiration, giving them fresh angles to explore.

Learning from those ahead on the path can energize them with new perspectives, quenching their thirst for knowledge while giving structure to keep going.

Managing Emotional Well-Being

Self-improvement is not just about external achievements. Emotional stability, stress management, and resilience also matter:

Stress Relief Habits: Activities like gentle stretches, nature walks, or quiet reflection can help calm the mind. The Archer might prefer short bursts of relaxation rather than long, formal sessions.

Mindful Pauses: Checking in with their emotions daily—asking themselves, "How do I feel right now?"—keeps them from burying stress under constant movement.

Sharing Feelings with Trusted Friends: While Sagittarians are direct, they might skip discussing deep personal struggles. Opening up can relieve internal pressure, improving mental health.

Accepting Self-Setbacks: If they deviate from a plan, they should resist harsh self-criticism. Recognizing that missteps are part of progress ensures they do not drop everything after a minor failure.

Nurturing emotional strength can be just as crucial as learning new skills, since it underpins how well they maintain momentum in the long run.

Healthy Lifestyle Choices

Physical well-being supports self-improvement. Sagittarius, with its energetic drive, often enjoys activity but might skip consistent routines. Some ideas:

Varied Exercise Routines: Rotating sports or activities—like yoga, badminton, brisk walking—fuels their excitement. A personal tracker or friend group can encourage consistency.

Balanced Eating: They might try new, interesting recipes so healthy meals never feel dull. Involving cultural dishes from different countries can suit their curiosity.

Adequate Sleep: It might be tempting to stay up reading about new topics, but regular rest improves focus and mood, fueling the next day's self-improvement tasks.

Mindful Treats: Occasional indulgences are fine, but the key is balance. Celebrating small victories with a treat is okay as long as it does not derail overall health.

A healthy body supports a sharp mind, giving Sagittarians the vitality to chase their goals and adapt to new challenges.

Continuous Learning and Skill Expansion

Learning new subjects or skills is a natural extension for Sagittarius. Formal or informal, it can take many forms:

Online Courses: Platforms that offer short video lessons on anything from coding to baking can keep them engaged. They can switch topics once they feel mastery or interest wanes.

Workshops and Seminars: If in-person events exist locally, a day or weekend workshop offers hands-on fun without a long-term commitment.

Book Clubs with Focus: A small group reading about topics like history, science, or personal finance can open them to deeper discussions.

Language Exchanges: Trying out foreign tongues can be thrilling, especially if they hope to travel or connect with people abroad.

They can plan a modest learning schedule—like devoting certain hours per week to a chosen topic—yet still remain flexible if a new subject grabs their interest.

Creating a Personal Improvement Plan

Though Sagittarians may shy away from rigid plans, having an outline can guide them. A plan could include:

1. **Core Goals:** e.g., "Learn intermediate Spanish," "Improve public speaking," "Gain better financial habits."

2. **Flexible Schedules:** e.g., "Study Spanish three times a week, 30 minutes each, on whichever days fit my routine."

3. **Progress Checkpoints:** e.g., "By next month, hold a basic conversation in Spanish."

4. **Reward System:** e.g., "When I complete a speech practice session, I'll watch a fun show or meet a friend."

5. **Review and Adjust:** Perhaps at the end of each month, they reflect on what worked, what bored them, and what can be tweaked.

Such an approach merges freedom with a sense of direction.

Motivating Factors for Sagittarius

Sagittarians can sustain motivation if they tie their improvements to something that sparks joy or curiosity. Examples:

Working Toward a Trip: If they want to visit a certain region, learning the local language or culture can keep them excited about daily study.

Sharing Knowledge with Others: Knowing they will present new findings to a group or teach a friend can push them to prepare thoroughly.

Aligning with Personal Philosophy: If they believe in broad-minded living, they might volunteer or join activism that fits their values, learning new organizational or leadership skills in the process.

Envisioning Future Adventures: Picturing themselves in a new role—like a confident speaker, a skillful artist, or a capable entrepreneur—can stoke their internal fire to keep practicing.

Building a strong emotional link to each goal helps them avoid dropping it when novelty fades.

Handling Impostor Feelings and Doubt

Even an upbeat Sagittarius can face self-doubt or feel like a beginner among experts. Strategies to manage that:

Embrace the Learner Role: Recognizing that every expert was once new can ease the shame of not knowing everything right away.

Ask Questions Freely: Sagittarians are often good at asking direct questions, so they can harness that to learn quickly without apology.

Celebrate Small Milestones: Acknowledging each step of progress, no matter how small, builds confidence that they are indeed improving.

Stay Realistic: Aiming for big leaps in a short time can create pressure. Balanced expectations maintain motivation.

Feeling uncertain does not mean they lack ability; it is a sign they are stretching into fresh territory, which suits the Archer's longing for exploration.

Strengthening Relationships as Self-Improvement

Personal growth is not solely about skills or intellect. Sagittarians can also hone how they connect with others:

Active Listening Practice: Working on giving friends or family the spotlight, truly hearing them before jumping in. This can deepen bonds.

Developing Empathy: Reading books on emotional intelligence or practicing calm support during friends' tough times fosters emotional maturity.

Conflict Resolution Growth: From Chapter 17, applying calm speech, fairness, and open-mindedness can be a personal skill they choose to refine.

Better relationships, in turn, give them more support and feedback, fueling a positive cycle of self-improvement.

Time Management Tools

A common struggle is that Sagittarians might enjoy spontaneous living, but effective self-improvement often needs some structure. Tools that strike a balance:

Digital Calendars with Color Coding: They can place tasks into broad categories—learning, health, social—and pick times that feel comfortable.

Task Apps with Gentle Reminders: Setting a daily or weekly nudge can help them remember tasks without an overwhelming alarm or strict schedule.

Bullet Journals or Quick Lists: A creative approach to journaling can spark excitement. They can doodle, add quotes, or track accomplishments in a visually appealing way.

"Time Blocking" in Loose Blocks: For instance, "Morning block: creativity," "Afternoon block: chores/work," "Evening block: social or relaxation," letting them decide specifics day by day.

These tactics help ensure self-improvement stays on their radar without making them feel micromanaged by their own plan.

Celebrating Progress in Meaningful Ways

Recognizing achievements is crucial so they see how far they have come. Examples:

- **Personal Journals of Highlights:** Writing a short entry about what they accomplished each week or month.

- **Shared Updates with Friends:** Telling a close circle what they've achieved, like finishing a small online course. This can spark encouraging feedback.

- **Symbolic Tokens:** Some people like to place small tokens (like stickers or badges) on a board each time they hit a milestone.

- **Doing Something Special:** They might treat themselves to an interesting experience or new book that aligns with their goal after reaching a benchmark.

This keeps morale high and encourages them to stick with the process, reinforcing the benefits of consistent effort.

Reinventing Goals if Motivation Fades

Sagittarius thrives on variety, so goals set a few months ago might lose appeal. That is not always a reason to quit; it could mean:

Refresh the Approach: If learning a language via textbooks feels dull, they might switch to conversational apps, real-life practice, or cultural immersion.

Refine the Goal: If "Read 50 books" seems uninspiring halfway through, maybe shift it to "Read about topics that fascinate me, at least 20 pages a day."

Combine Goals with Existing Passions: If they are bored with standard workout routines, they might join a sports group or try something adventurous like rock climbing (safely).

Pause, Then Resume Later: Sometimes a short break to explore a new interest can reignite the original spark down the line.

Being flexible ensures they do not force themselves into a dead-end routine, but also do not abandon all progress at the first hint of boredom.

Using Travel as a Self-Improvement Tool

Many Sagittarians love to travel, which can become a catalyst for growth. Traveling helps them:

Learn Cultural Sensitivity: Interacting with different ways of life can boost empathy and global awareness.

Practice Problem-Solving: Navigating unfamiliar places hones adaptability, a skill that translates back home.

Build Confidence: Overcoming language barriers or planning a trip fosters a sense of capability.

Spark New Interests: Observing local crafts, art, or traditions might open a new hobby or career path.

They can set improvement goals tied to travel, such as learning basic phrases before going abroad or writing travel journals that track personal insights gained on each trip.

Handling Overwhelm or Burnout

Sometimes, in pursuit of many goals, a Sagittarius might overdo it, piling on too many tasks. Burnout signals might include fatigue, irritability, or losing enjoyment. Strategies to cope:

Prioritize Ruthlessly: Temporarily set aside less essential goals to focus on the main ones.

Schedule Relaxation: Ironically, planning free time can help them truly disconnect without guilt.

Say "No" Where Needed: If they have too many responsibilities, politely declining extra tasks or events protects their energy.

Check Emotional Warning Signs: If they feel consistently anxious or low, it might be time to lighten the load. They could discuss it with a friend or counselor to prevent serious burnout.

Remembering that self-improvement is a marathon, not a sprint, helps them maintain a healthy pace.

Transforming Mistakes Into Growth

Because Sagittarians can be impulsive, mistakes may happen along the way. Instead of feeling defeated:

Reflect Briefly, Then Move On: Dwelling on errors can drain motivation. A quick reflection on what went wrong helps them do better next time.

Extract Lessons: Asking themselves, "What can I learn from this slip-up?" reframes it as part of progress.

Share the Story: If they feel comfortable, telling a friend or mentor about the misstep can lead to fresh insights and support.

Stay Humble, Stay Curious: Recognizing that mistakes are signs they are experimenting can keep them open to new attempts.

This approach aligns with the Archer's ability to bounce back, turning stumbles into stepping stones.

Welcoming Feedback

Sagittarians often give honest feedback to others, but receiving it can be equally important for self-improvement. They can:

Ask Specific Questions: Instead of, "What do you think?" they might say, "Could you tell me which parts of my presentation felt unclear?"

Take a Calm Moment Before Responding: If feedback feels harsh, a short pause prevents defensive reactions.

Implement What Resonates: They can note down suggestions and see which ones align with their goals. Not all feedback must be used, but an open mind helps.

Thank the Person: Even if they do not fully agree, acknowledging the effort fosters a positive environment for future input.

Learning to accept others' viewpoints polishes the Archer's communication and fosters deeper relationships.

Creating a Supportive Environment

Self-improvement stands on firmer ground when the Sagittarius shapes an environment that sparks curiosity and comfort:

Organized but Inspiring Workspace: They can keep supplies or tools (like a guitar, art kit, or language apps) easily accessible in a pleasant corner. Add bright colors or travel photos for motivation.

Tech That Simplifies: Using user-friendly apps or online platforms that track progress can reduce the headache of remembering everything.

Supportive Social Circle: Spending time with people who respect their aspirations can fuel positive momentum. Encouragers who also try new things can keep them enthusiastic.

Limiting Negative Influences: If certain circles mock or belittle self-improvement attempts, a Sagittarius might reduce time spent there, focusing on healthier dynamics.

Shaping an environment that aligns with their cheerful, inquisitive nature makes daily efforts smoother and more fun.

Embracing the Long-Term Mindset

A major hurdle is that Sagittarians often crave quick excitement. Yet deeper transformations—like mastering a skill, building emotional resilience, or shaping a fulfilling career—take time:

Break Down Major Goals: Splitting a big objective (for instance, writing a novel) into smaller phases (outline, draft chapters, revise) keeps them moving steadily.

Focus on Process Over Immediate Results: They can watch for mini improvements—like writing more fluid sentences or hitting the right note in singing—rather than expecting instant mastery.

Rotate Projects in Cycles: If a single focus bores them, they might schedule certain weeks for one project, then rotate to another, ensuring variety while gradually advancing each goal.

Acknowledge that Growth Is Ongoing: Even after reaching a milestone, there is always more to learn or refine. The Archer who embraces lifelong learning stays energized.

By seeing self-improvement as an evolving endeavor, they reduce the pressure for instant success and keep their spark alive.

Celebrating Accomplishments with Others

Sharing progress can solidify the sense of achievement:

Host a Small Gathering: For a big milestone, inviting a few friends or colleagues for a casual meetup can highlight the success.

Showcase Skills: For instance, if they learned to play guitar, performing a short piece at a friend's house might be fulfilling.

Gift Themselves Something Useful: Perhaps a new tool, book, or software that supports the next step of improvement.

When Sagittarians share these moments, they also inspire others. This mutual exchange of encouragement can spark fresh ideas for everyone involved.

Integrating Self-Improvement Into Daily Life

Instead of viewing self-improvement as a separate box, Sagittarians can weave it into everyday routines:

Habit Stacking: Attach a new habit to an existing one. For example, after making morning coffee, practice vocabulary words for five minutes.

Brief Practice Intervals: Insert small skill reviews during lunch breaks, commutes (like listening to language podcasts), or before bed.

Social Accountability: If meeting a friend for lunch, they might discuss each other's progress in a friendly manner, turning casual chats into motivational check-ins.

At-Home Experiments: Cooking dinner can become a skill-building session if they try new recipes or techniques. The everyday act of preparing meals then doubles as a self-improvement zone.

This approach lessens the feeling that improvement is a heavy add-on. It becomes part of their vibrant, day-to-day life.

CHAPTER 19: SAGITTARIUS IN GROUPS

Sagittarians are often seen as bright, outgoing, and open to meeting people. They can bring a lively spark to group settings, whether it's a casual club, a friend circle, or a professional team. However, being part of a group also means sharing responsibilities, respecting boundaries, and adjusting to different personalities. In this chapter, we will look at how Sagittarians behave when they join or form groups, what strengths they bring, and what challenges might arise. We will not repeat major details from earlier chapters; instead, we will explore fresh insights into how the Archer style adapts to teamwork, friendship circles, clubs, or community projects.

Embracing the Group Experience

Sagittarians generally enjoy social contact. They can thrive in shared efforts if they feel free to contribute ideas without getting bogged down by overly strict rules. A group environment, in many ways, suits their preference for lively interaction and learning from various viewpoints. When stepping into a new group, they often:

Bring Curiosity: They tend to ask questions, eager to understand the group's purpose.

Offer Friendly Greetings: Sagittarians usually extend warm welcomes to people they have just met, helping break any initial tension.

Scan for Possibilities: They might say, "Have we thought of doing this differently?" soon after joining, reflecting their desire to add fresh ideas.

However, they may also want to keep some personal independence. For instance, if the group expects everyone to follow a strict process, the Sagittarius could feel stifled, resulting in restlessness or partial withdrawal.

Sagittarius Strengths in Group Settings

When Sagittarians enter a team, club, or community circle, certain positive traits often stand out:

Enthusiasm and Energy: They lift morale by bringing an upbeat approach. Others may feel motivated to try new things or see fresh angles.

Openness to Discussion: They enjoy hearing different opinions, so group members often feel comfortable contributing. The Sagittarius can moderate free-flowing talks, making sure no single perspective is ignored.

Idea Generation: Sagittarians often propose innovative concepts. Whether it's a fresh project step or a creative event theme, they spark brainstorming sessions that can lead to breakthroughs.

Adaptability: They handle unexpected changes well. If a plan shifts abruptly, Sagittarians quickly pivot, maintaining a hopeful outlook that keeps everyone else calm.

Because of these traits, they can be a welcome addition to groups that need a shot of excitement or a broader view.

Potential Challenges in Group Environments

Yet, certain Sagittarius qualities might cause friction if not managed thoughtfully:

Impatience with Details: If the group project calls for careful, step-by-step tasks, the Sagittarius may grow bored or rush, risking errors.

Blurting Out Opinions: Their directness can be taken as criticism if they do not phrase feedback gently. Group members with sensitive temperaments might feel hurt by blunt remarks.

Jumping Between Roles: A Sagittarius might volunteer for multiple sub-tasks, only to realize they have too much on their plate. The group could then face confusion if tasks remain unfinished.

Restlessness Under Rigid Schedules: Groups that have many rules or extended formal meetings might see the Sagittarius tune out or try to change the format to be more flexible.

Balancing enthusiasm and courtesy, and remembering that thoroughness sometimes matters, can help the Archer avoid these pitfalls.

Joining Existing Groups vs. Starting New Ones

A Sagittarius might join an existing team or create a group from scratch:

Joining an Existing Team: At first, they can observe the group's structure and unwritten norms. After an initial period, they will likely propose adjustments or fresh projects. If the group appreciates new energy, this goes smoothly. If it resists change, tensions may flare.

Forming a New Group: This scenario can be exciting for the Archer, who can shape the group's purpose and style from the start. They might invite diverse members, setting a relaxed yet goal-oriented tone. However, they must still ensure some order is in place, or the group might drift without direction.

In either case, listening to others' opinions is key. While the Sagittarius can spark a group into action, they also need buy-in from fellow members.

Leadership Roles for Sagittarius

Sagittarians often find themselves in leadership or influencer positions, not always by conscious choice but because of their natural confidence and bright energy. In a leadership role, they might:

Inspire Others: By expressing a big-picture view, they encourage the group to aim high.

Foster Open Communication: They usually invite team members to share opinions freely, increasing group creativity.

Offer Quick Solutions: They can propose fast fixes for immediate problems. This agility helps keep projects moving.

Yet, a Sagittarius leader must watch out for:

Overpromising: In their optimism, they might commit the group to ambitious objectives without thinking through logistics.

Skipping Follow-Through: If they dislike details, someone else on the team must handle final checks. Otherwise, tasks may remain partially done.

Handling Disputes: Chapter 17 talked about conflict. As a leader, the Sagittarius must keep calm, carefully listening to all sides, not just pushing a personal vision.

A balanced approach—mixing inspiration with organization—keeps their leadership effective.

Contributing as a Team Player

Not all Sagittarians want to lead. Sometimes, they prefer contributing specific skills while staying flexible. As a team member, they can:

Support Brainstorming: The Archer can push the group to think in new directions.

Take on Lively Tasks: They might handle roles requiring interaction, such as public outreach, social media engagement, or event planning.

Mediate Light Conflict: Their direct style can cut through misunderstandings if used tactfully—"Let's clarify what each person meant."

Challenges might surface if the group demands tasks the Sagittarius finds tedious, like extended data entry. By agreeing to share responsibilities or rotate tasks with others, they avoid burnout while keeping the group functional.

Handling Group Dynamics

Each group has distinct dynamics shaped by personalities, goals, and unspoken norms. Sagittarians can watch for:

Dominant Personalities: The Archer might clash if another strong-willed individual tries to squash new ideas. The key is calm but firm communication.

Slow Decision-Makers: Some members might need more time to reflect. A Sagittarius can practice patience, trusting that not everyone jumps into action as fast as they do.

Hidden Tensions: Because Sagittarians value honesty, they might sense frustration beneath polite smiles. Bringing issues into the open can solve problems early, but they must do it gently.

Group Fatigue: If morale dips due to repeated setbacks, a Sagittarius can step in with encouraging words or a fun approach to lighten the mood and refocus on solutions.

By tuning in to these patterns, the Archer can adapt and help build harmony, making the group more cohesive.

Projects and Events That Suit Sagittarius

Groups often form around a task or shared interest. Sagittarians usually thrive in groups that align with their love of exploration, communication, or variety:

Travel Clubs: If the group organizes day trips or vacations, a Sagittarius might be the energetic planner, suggesting lesser-known destinations.

Culture and Art Communities: They can help arrange cultural fairs, art collaborations, or music events, adding flair and creative marketing ideas.

Charity or Volunteer Teams: Many Sagittarians feel a moral urge to assist. They might enjoy short-term volunteer projects that offer direct impact, like food drives or local fundraisers.

Workshop or Learning Circles: If the group studies languages, new skills, or shares knowledge, the Sagittarius can keep discussions lively and inclusive.

Such settings harness the Archer's optimism and willingness to try new methods, encouraging productive outcomes.

Balancing Independence with Collective Goals

A central theme for Sagittarians in groups is balancing personal autonomy with the group's collective aims:

Agreeing on Common Rules: Even if they dislike too many constraints, Sagittarians can support a few guidelines to help the group stay on track, provided those rules make sense.

Taking Breaks If Needed: If they feel smothered, stepping away for a short interval or focusing on individual tasks can refresh their enthusiasm.

Offering Flexible Roles: They might propose a rotating system, so no one is stuck in the same job for too long. This encourages variety and suits the Sagittarius style.

Checking in on Others: The Archer can sometimes become absorbed in their own ideas. Taking time to ask group mates about their tasks fosters unity and mutual support.

This approach preserves the Sagittarian sense of freedom without undermining teamwork.

Social Gatherings and Friend Circles

Outside of formal teams, Sagittarians often participate in friend groups, where their personality can shine:

Hosting Group Hangouts: They might invite friends to casual parties, game nights, or potluck dinners, always adding a creative twist—like a themed playlist or a small quiz to spark conversation.

Suggesting Outdoor Activities: Because many Sagittarians prefer open spaces, they might rally friends for a day at the park, a mild hike, or a sports match.

Arranging Cultural Exchanges: Sharing foreign films, local cultural nights, or interesting discussion topics can draw the group closer.

Challenges appear if friends expect them to handle too many logistics. A Sagittarius might be an amazing idea generator but less thrilled about setting up chairs or handling budget details. Delegating tasks among friends helps keep them from feeling overwhelmed.

Conflict Within a Group

Groups are not immune to disagreements. As Chapter 17 detailed, Sagittarians can bring clarity to conflict if they manage their blunt side. In group settings:

Address Tension Early: The Archer's directness can help the group name the issue instead of letting resentment fester. They can say, "I sense we're not aligned. Let's discuss it now."

Encourage Open Dialogue: They might propose a structured talk where each person briefly shares concerns, ensuring no single voice dominates.

Offer Mutual Solutions: Sagittarians can remind members that the goal is a win-win approach. They might ask, "How can each of us modify our approach so we move forward together?"

Stay Respectful: Using calm, considerate language is crucial. If the Sagittarius becomes too forceful, it could escalate the conflict instead.

When done well, their honesty and optimism can turn group conflicts into beneficial realignments.

Motivating a Group

Sagittarians often excel at lifting spirits. They can help a group keep excitement alive through:

Fun Challenges or Games: Whether it's a quick team-building activity or a small friendly contest, adding playful elements makes tasks more engaging.

Positive Future Vision: They might remind the group of the bigger picture or end goal, reigniting everyone's enthusiasm.

Storytelling: Sharing short anecdotes of past successes or humorous mishaps can build camaraderie, showing that adversity is normal but surmountable.

Light Rewards for Milestones: Though the Archer might avoid overly formal systems, small gestures—like bringing snacks or praising a job well done—boost morale.

By blending creativity with support, they keep momentum high, ensuring group members do not feel the project is just a dull chore.

Handling Overcommitment

Sagittarians may join multiple groups or volunteer for several roles at once, drawn by diverse interests. Overcommitment can strain them and cause letdowns for the groups expecting their presence.

Strategies to avoid this:

Choose Key Activities: Assess which groups genuinely ignite passion. Limit membership in those that merely sound mildly appealing.

Set Realistic Time Blocks: They might say, "I can only attend two weekly meetings, so I'll pick the ones that matter most."

Communicate Clearly: If they need to scale back, telling the group in advance is better than dropping out last minute.

Delegate or Rotate: If they have a leadership role, delegating smaller tasks prevents them from carrying the entire burden alone.

By focusing energy on fewer, more meaningful groups, Sagittarians can maintain quality participation without burnout.

Cultural or International Groups

Many Sagittarians enjoy cross-cultural involvement. For instance, an international student club, a global volunteer project, or an online forum with diverse members. In such settings, their traits can blossom:

Global Curiosity: They embrace learning from people of different backgrounds, bridging cultural gaps.

Tolerance and Openness: They often champion inclusive communication, encouraging others to share unique customs or viewpoints.

Enthusiastic Event Planning: They might suggest multicultural food festivals or language exchange nights, showcasing their flair for variety.

Pitfalls can arise if they speak too freely in environments where certain topics are sensitive. Adapting to cultural norms while staying genuine is vital.

Professional Networking and Conferences

Sagittarians can also show strength in professional gatherings or conferences:

Approachable Networking: They approach new contacts with a friendly attitude, quickly building rapport.

Asking Engaging Questions: At industry panels or workshops, they might spark group discussions by inquiring about broader trends or real-life examples.

Proposing Collaborations: If they sense synergy between different professionals, they enjoy connecting them, facilitating partnerships.

However, they must keep track of follow-up steps. Collecting business cards or making initial agreements is helpful only if they follow through with messages or set actual meetings to explore collaborative ideas.

Virtual Groups and Online Communities

Digital networks are abundant: social media groups, discussion forums, gaming guilds, or online study sessions. Sagittarians can flourish online, but certain issues might surface:

Too Many Distractions: Browsing multiple groups can dilute their focus. They might skip crucial conversations or tasks if they spread themselves too thin.

Rapid Tone Misinterpretation: Their blunt text could be misunderstood. Emojis or polite disclaimers can help clarify friendly intent.

Keeping Commitments: Online communities sometimes hold group events at specific times. A Sagittarian should mark the schedule to avoid missing them if they want to be reliable.

By joining a manageable number of virtual groups and engaging thoughtfully, they can enjoy global connections without feeling flooded by constant pings.

Setting Group Goals and Schedules

When a Sagittarius is heavily involved in group planning, balancing structure with flexibility can benefit everyone:

Define Broad Objectives: "Our aim is to raise funds for a local charity within the next two months," or "We want to host three cultural events this semester."

Keep Timelines Realistic: Instead of daily check-ins, maybe a weekly or biweekly meeting suits the Archer's style.

Embrace Adaptive Plans: The group might detail certain tasks but remain open to alternative approaches if new ideas arise.

Document Agreements: A basic shared online document or short meeting notes ensure that no one forgets the group's decisions.

Such structures help the group function efficiently without boxing in the Sagittarian spirit.

Encouraging a Sense of Community

Groups often flourish when members feel connected. A Sagittarius can foster community by:

Arranging Casual Social Time: Even if the group is work-focused, having a small informal chat or a brief snack break fosters camaraderie.

Recognizing Achievements: If someone completes a tough sub-task, giving a public nod can lift group morale.

Organizing Rotational Hosting: For in-person gatherings, they might propose rotating who hosts. Sagittarians can add a fun twist each time.

Highlighting Personal Interests: Encouraging members to share a hobby or fun fact about themselves allows deeper bonds beyond the group's main activity.

Because they enjoy friendly interaction, Sagittarians naturally help create a lively atmosphere that keeps people engaged on more than just tasks.

Collaboration Styles That Suit Sagittarius

In more formal group collaborations—like business ventures or large creative projects—Sagittarians might:

Gravitate Toward Idea or People Roles: They excel in brainstorming, promoting, or forging new contacts.

Request Flexible Task Assignments: Instead of doing the same function for months, they may rotate tasks to maintain enthusiasm.

Stay Clear of Overly Detailed Lab Work: If the project demands intense focus on narrow details for extended periods, they may get restless. Pairing them with detail-oriented partners can balance the group.

Communicate Frequently and Casually: Quick check-ins, friendly group chats, or voice calls can feel more natural to them than heavy formal reports.

Both the Archer and the group benefit if they place Sagittarians where their spontaneity and broad perspective shine, while letting others manage the detail-heavy elements.

Building Long-Term Connections

After a project ends or a club wraps up, Sagittarians may want to stay in touch if the experience was positive. Maintaining these connections can lead to lifelong friendships or future collaborations. They can:

Exchange Personal Updates: Drop the occasional message about how they are doing, or ask about the other person's progress.

Meet Up Periodically: They might propose small reunions or side projects, capitalizing on the earlier group synergy.

Keep an Eye on Opportunities: If they see an interesting event that aligns with a past group's interests, they can share it, reminding members of their bond.

Celebrate Shared Memories: Posting group photos or short reflections on what they accomplished fosters a sense of pride.

Sustaining these links can bring fresh chances to learn or collaborate down the road.

Handling Group Burnout

Groups can face burnout if members have worked together for a long period with few breaks or too many repetitive tasks. A Sagittarius noticing signs of group fatigue can:

Suggest Fun Mini-Breaks: A short collective pause for a simple game, comedic video, or personal story exchange lifts spirits.

Rotate Roles: If certain people are stuck in the same tasks, trying new roles can re-energize them.

Introduce a New Angle: A small pivot in the group's approach might rekindle curiosity—like experimenting with different methods to achieve goals.

Balance Realism with Positivity: They can acknowledge the stress while also reminding everyone about the purpose of the project, renewing motivation.

By combining empathy with their optimistic spark, Sagittarians help groups push through fatigue toward renewed engagement.

Large Gatherings and Conferences

Beyond small teams, Sagittarians might also attend or organize large gatherings—like annual conferences, festivals, or multi-day symposiums. In these settings, they can:

Serve as Enthusiastic Hosts or Moderators: The Archer's comfort with public speaking and spontaneity can energize crowds.

Network Across Many Booths or Panels: They jump between different sessions, gleaning wide knowledge and forging multiple connections.

Propose Lively Side Activities: Large gatherings sometimes need informal events. Sagittarians might arrange a casual meetup, an evening get-together, or an open mic for participants.

Boost Overall Atmosphere: By greeting strangers openly, they spread a welcoming vibe that helps attendees feel at ease.

They just need to manage time well, or they risk missing scheduled tasks amid the event's bustling pace.

Learning from Group Experiences

Each group setting can teach a Sagittarius valuable lessons about collaboration, leadership, and empathy. After the group project or event concludes, reflecting can help them grow:

Identify Personal Strengths: Were they best at generating new ideas, motivating others, or bridging conflicts?

Spot Weak Points: Did they forget deadlines, overwhelm themselves, or talk over quieter members? Recognizing these tendencies can guide future improvements.

Gather Feedback: Asking for honest opinions from other members fosters insight, especially if the Archer wants to refine their group interaction style.

Apply Lessons Forward: They can tweak their approach next time—for instance, giving more space for detail-oriented steps or scheduling short but regular check-ins.

This reflective practice transforms each group experience into a stepping stone for stronger interpersonal skills.

Creating a Balanced Group Life

If they love social engagement, a Sagittarius might juggle multiple group activities: a volunteer team, a friend circle that meets for board games, and a professional committee at work. While this can be fulfilling, it risks stress or shallow involvement if they spread themselves too thin. Balancing it all:

Set Clear Priorities: Decide which group truly needs consistent attention and which can be visited occasionally.

Allocate Different Times: For example, volunteer on weekends, attend the friend circle once every other week, and attend the professional committee's monthly meeting.

Avoid Overlapping Commitments: If two groups meet at the same time, the Sagittarius might have to pick one consistently or rotate attendance.

Stay Honest with Each Group: Let them know how much time you can realistically invest, so no one feels let down.

By organizing schedules and communicating openly, they ensure each group gets the best of their involvement rather than leftover scraps of attention.

CHAPTER 20: SAGITTARIUS AND FUTURE PLANS

Sagittarians are famed for looking at broad horizons. They often focus on what might come next, brimming with excitement about new discoveries. For this final chapter, we will discuss how Sagittarians approach the future—shaping long-range plans, juggling hopes and practicalities, and learning to handle unpredictability without losing their spark. We will not rehash earlier material in depth, but rather bring fresh insights on how the Archer can channel optimism into meaningful forward steps, from career choices and personal visions to broader life changes. This chapter also covers ways to handle anxiety about the unknown, plus tips for staying balanced and grounded while forging ahead.

Sagittarius and the Call of the Future

Sagittarians carry a sense that life is full of open doors. They might see each day as a chance to find something fresh or sharpen their talents. When thinking about what lies ahead, they typically:

Imagine Many Paths: They are open to multiple scenarios, rarely locking themselves into one plan from an early stage.

Embrace Hope: They believe improvements or breakthroughs are always possible. This can motivate them to push forward.

Expect Surprises: Instead of fearing twists, they often see them as potential adventures.

However, strong optimism alone does not ensure success. Detailed steps and consistent efforts still matter, especially for bigger undertakings like building a career, setting up a home, or saving funds for retirement. Balancing grand visions with daily discipline is often the core challenge for the Archer.

Setting Long-Term Goals

Sagittarians can craft meaningful goals if they are truly invested. For instance:

Career Growth or Change: They might aim for a promotion, pivot into a different industry, or start a side business that aligns with their interests.

Personal Development: Long-term aims like mastering a foreign language or writing a book can drive them to learn steadily.

Travel or Cultural Exploration: Many set future objectives tied to seeing particular lands, volunteering abroad, or engaging in cross-cultural projects.

Community Impact: Some might want to support local charities, run for a community board, or expand a volunteer initiative.

The key is clarifying what excites them enough to overcome routine tasks required for achieving it. Because a Sagittarian might dream about many directions, focusing on a few that truly resonate is crucial.

Approaches to Career Planning

Sagittarians frequently change jobs or fields if they get bored or sense a better opportunity. They are not afraid of fresh starts. Nonetheless, they should consider:

Exploring Options Without Burning Bridges: If they plan to leave a role, doing so respectfully—finishing projects, giving notice—helps maintain positive references.

Identifying Transferable Skills: Whether they have strong communication ability, leadership potential, or idea generation, these can apply to new jobs, softening the risk of shifting careers.

Setting Benchmarks: Even if they enjoy spontaneity, marking certain points—like "In one year, I want to upgrade my professional certifications"—keeps them from drifting.

Seeking Mentors: Talking to those in desired fields can shorten the learning curve. Mentors can offer perspective on whether the new direction aligns with the Sagittarius's talents.

When done thoughtfully, a flexible career path can be an asset for them, allowing continuous learning without endless trial-and-error or abrupt changes that hamper stability.

Financial and Practical Preparation

While Sagittarians often focus on big ideas, practical life elements—such as budgeting, saving, or property decisions—cannot be ignored. They can maintain their spontaneity while still building security:

Setting Basic Financial Goals: For example, saving a set portion of income each month for emergencies, travel funds, or a future house.

Using Simple Tools: They might enjoy apps that track spending automatically, reducing the tedium of manual entries.

Avoiding Impulsive Large Purchases: Checking in with themselves—"Does this align with my bigger plan?"—before big spending can curb regrets.

Seeking Advice if Needed: A quick chat with a financial coach or a savvy friend helps them shape a plan that does not feel too strict but offers stability.

This framework creates a cushion for future endeavors, letting them adapt to unexpected events without panic.

Personal Life and Family Plans

Some Sagittarians may want a traditional family structure, while others prefer a more flexible arrangement. In either scenario, considering the future helps:

Discussing Goals with a Partner: If they want kids or a specific living arrangement, open talks prevent misunderstandings. A partner might need more certainty than the Archer typically offers.

Balancing Freedom and Domestic Life: With children or a spouse, certain routines become necessary. A Sagittarius can propose fun family activities or flexible holiday trips, keeping life interesting for all.

Exploring Non-Traditional Paths: They might choose co-living communities, extended travel while home-schooling kids, or other arrangements that reflect their wide outlook.

Planning for Aging Family Members: If they have older relatives to care for in the future, factoring that into plans now can avert sudden stress later.

Even if they do not see themselves in a typical household, a basic roadmap can reduce future conflicts or burdens.

Dealing with Uncertainty and Anxiety

For all their hopefulness, Sagittarians can still feel uneasy about big unknowns—like economic changes, global shifts, or personal health concerns. Handling that:

Stay Informed Reasonably: They can read reliable sources to keep track of trends without flooding themselves with worry.

Focus on Adaptable Skills: Building diverse capabilities ensures they can pivot in uncertain conditions.

Practice Small Stress-Relief Routines: A short daily reflection, breath exercise, or simple physical activity keeps tension in check.

Use Optimism Wisely: They might remind themselves that obstacles are not permanent, but also back it up with practical steps to navigate them.

This balance of positivity and realism helps them remain flexible, trusting they can handle change without ignoring real hazards.

Education and Lifelong Learning

Some Sagittarians keep returning to school or training programs. Their thirst for knowledge can shape future plans:

Pursuing Advanced Degrees: If it aligns with career or personal interest, they may enjoy graduate studies or specialized certifications.

Online Learning Platforms: In a fast-changing world, short online courses can be their gateway to new fields. They can pick and choose classes that match evolving goals.

Self-Directed Study Projects: They might set up a personal reading schedule, research diaries, or skill challenges, letting them explore new topics at their own pace.

Combining Travel and Learning: Studying abroad or attending global seminars satisfies both curiosity and wanderlust.

By integrating these options, Sagittarians keep their minds sharp, ensuring their future holds fresh intellectual ventures.

Potential Paths in Entrepreneurship

Some Sagittarians prefer to create their own work environment, forging businesses or ventures that reflect their interests. They might:

Launch a Start-Up: If they have an innovative idea or see a gap in the market, their passion can power early growth.

Freelance or Consultancy: Offering services in areas like writing, design, coaching, or marketing allows flexible hours, suiting their dislike of rigid schedules.

Combine Passions: For example, a travel blogger who also sells digital courses or organizes small tours. This merges personal curiosity with income.

Build Partnerships: The Archer can partner with detail-oriented individuals who keep track of finances and operations, balancing out their big-picture approach.

They should remember, though, that successful entrepreneurship needs dedication beyond initial excitement. Building a stable client base, managing budgets, and marketing consistently are key.

Philanthropy and Social Impact

As they look to the future, many Sagittarians want to leave a positive mark. They can:

Contribute to Causes: Donating time, skills, or money to charities or social projects. They might also champion an issue they feel strongly about, such as environmental preservation or educational access.

Create Nonprofit Initiatives: If they see a gap in their community, they might gather volunteers, plan events, or lead awareness campaigns, using their energy to mobilize support.

Involve Friends and Networks: They often excel at rallying people around a shared cause, especially if they show genuine passion and a welcoming spirit.

Making a difference satisfies their moral sense, adding depth to future plans beyond purely personal achievements.

Travel Dreams and Explorations

One hallmark of Sagittarius is love of travel. Their future plans might include:

Mapping a World Tour (or Smaller Adventures): Some dream of visiting several continents, absorbing diverse cultures.

Blending Travel with Work: Remote jobs, digital nomad lifestyles, or short international contracts can keep them on the move.

Volunteering Abroad: They may want to join overseas projects for a few months, combining service with cultural immersion.

Language and Cultural Goals: Setting the aim of speaking another language well enough to get by in daily life or diving into local art scenes can shape meaningful trips.

They just need to ensure financial and practical readiness, so these adventures do not become chaotic or draining.

Personal Growth Milestones

Future plans can also involve intangible growth. For instance:

Refining Emotional Intelligence: Some Sagittarians vow to be more patient, empathetic, or better listeners. They see it as a step to healthier relationships.

Developing Spiritual Perspectives: If spirituality or philosophical exploration matters to them, they might allocate time to read texts, join discussions, or practice mindful reflection.

Tackling Self-Limiting Habits: They might aim to reduce procrastination, manage impulses, or structure daily routines in a way that supports bigger goals.

Pursuing a Balanced Life: Setting marks for mental health check-ins, consistent exercise, or creative outlets helps them keep a well-rounded future.

These internal milestones can be just as vital as external achievements, ensuring they grow not only in skill but in self-awareness and emotional depth.

Handling Midlife and Life Transitions

Major transitions—like turning 30, 40, or 50, changing relationships, or shifting careers—can trigger reevaluation. Sagittarians might respond by:

Seeking Fresh Challenges: Instead of dreading a "midlife crisis," they might see it as a chance to start something new, like learning an instrument or taking a sabbatical.

Assessing Past Choices: A friendly reflection on achievements and regrets might prompt them to adjust future plans. They might conclude, for example, "I want to devote more time to creative writing now."

Redirecting Energies: If they have established a career, they might pivot to mentoring younger folks or exploring philanthropic routes.

Spreading Optimism to Others: They can serve as an example that life stages do not have to be limiting. Their typical boldness can show that big dreams can arise at any age.

By seeing transitions as doorways, they keep momentum even as life circumstances shift.

Retirement or Later Years

Retirement does not mean a total slowdown for many Sagittarians. They may plan:

Part-Time Consulting: Sharing expertise in a flexible format.

Travel Agenda: Visiting places they never had time for earlier.

Community Roles: Volunteering or teaching local classes, ensuring they remain socially involved.

Personal Passions: Immersing themselves in writing, painting, or any hobby that they once sidelined.

Balancing health care, financial stability, and continued excitement remains key. With planning, the Archer's later years can be filled with exploration rather than inactivity.

Embracing Spontaneous Opportunities

Despite the need for planning, Sagittarians want space for spur-of-the-moment choices. They might spot a unique event or short contract abroad and decide, "Yes, let's do it." To manage this blend of structure and spontaneity:

Keep a Fluid Calendar: Having a broad timeline with some open slots allows them to fit in unexpected events without wrecking other commitments.

Reserve a "Fun Fund:" Setting aside a bit of money monthly so they can afford last-minute trips or exciting local events guilt-free.

Maintain Basic Security Nets: As long as bills are covered and obligations are handled, a few leaps into unknown territory are less risky.

Communicate with Loved Ones: If they have family or close partners, explaining that they might take a short notice opportunity fosters understanding.

This approach honors their free spirit without causing chaos in their daily life.

Coping with Disappointment or Delays

Not all big ideas pan out smoothly. Sagittarians might face delays: a trip canceled, a startup that stumbles, or personal obstacles. They can address setbacks by:

Revisiting Core Motivation: Asking themselves, "Why did I want this in the first place?" can reignite determination if the goal is still valid.

Adapting Plans: If certain routes close, they might find alternate ways to reach the same end. This resilience suits their flexible mindset.

Seeking Support: Friends, mentors, or online groups can offer moral backing, brainstorming solutions or reminding them of prior successes.

Finding Lessons: Viewing a failed attempt as practice for the next idea helps them remain confident, ensuring they do not get stuck in discouragement.

An occasional letdown does not defeat a Sagittarius. Their typical response is to regroup and look for the next route forward.

Sustaining Optimism Over the Long Haul

Sagittarians are known for positivity, yet life's complexities can wear on anyone. Keeping morale high might include:

Small Celebrations of Progress: Marking mini-achievements in a way that feels rewarding.

Connecting with Like-Minded People: Surrounding themselves with encouraging folks who also see possibilities, preventing cynicism from taking root.

Using Humor as a Release: Light jokes or comedic breaks help them handle rough patches without losing hope.

Reflecting on Past Triumphs: Thinking about earlier times when they overcame obstacles to remind themselves they can do it again.

This consistent positivity is a hallmark of Sagittarius resilience, but it must be paired with practical action to remain grounded.

Sharing Their Vision with Others

Some Sagittarians have a big dream that involves a broader circle—maybe launching a community initiative or writing a book that impacts many. They can:

State the Vision Clearly: If they want others to join, describing the goal in vivid terms ignites interest.

Invite Collaboration: They might gather friends or experts who complement their skill gaps. This fosters collective ownership.

Stay Open to Input: While they can champion the vision, refining details based on feedback ensures it stays realistic.

Build a Timeline: Shared projects often need milestones. Even if flexible, having rough targets keeps everyone moving cohesively.

When they share future-oriented ideas wholeheartedly, Sagittarians can inspire entire teams or communities, echoing the sign's capacity to motivate beyond personal gain.

Avoiding the Trap of Endless Daydreaming

Though Sagittarians love planning big things, daydreaming can become an escape if no actual steps follow.

To avoid drifting:

Prioritize Two or Three Major Dreams: Focusing energies there prevents scattering across dozens of half-formed aims.

Take Real Action Quickly: Even a tiny move—like sending an inquiry email or researching a course—transforms a dream into a practical start.

Set Deadlines for Planning: The Archer might say, "Within two weeks, I'll finalize my approach for this project," preventing indefinite pondering.

Measure Progress Regularly: Checking what was accomplished each month ensures daydreams translate into forward motion.

They can keep the imaginative spark alive, but ground it in consistent movement, reining in the danger of "all talk, no action."

Navigating Technology and Social Changes

As the world evolves rapidly, Sagittarians might see countless new tools, career trends, or social shifts that affect future paths. They can:

Embrace Ongoing Learning: Keeping an eye on emerging tech or social media platforms ensures they stay relevant in professional or creative fields.

Blend Old and New: Using technology but also preserving authentic face-to-face interactions suits the Archer's desire for broad experiences.

Stay Ethical: Considering how new trends impact communities or the environment aligns with the moral side many Sagittarians feel.

Experiment with Platforms: They might try digital channels for self-expression—podcasts, vlogs, or webinars—while still trusting personal instincts on which ones resonate best.

This openness to modern shifts keeps them flexible and able to pivot future plans if global conditions change.

Inspiring Others to Plan for the Future

Sagittarians often act as motivators for friends, relatives, or coworkers who feel stuck. They can:

Encourage Brainstorm Sessions: Helping others see potential paths, using that famous Archer vision.

Offer Practical Optimism: Balancing hopeful words with reminders that small steps lead to big goals.

Provide Honest Feedback: If a friend's plan seems unrealistic, they might gently suggest adjustments rather than dismissing it outright.

Lead by Example: By steadily pursuing their own future objectives in a transparent, upbeat way, they show that forward-thinking can be both exciting and achievable.

Sharing this spirit of possibility transforms not only their own future but also the outlook of the people around them.

Self-Care Along the Way

While building tomorrow, Sagittarians must remember self-care in the present. Overextending themselves is easy if they chase many dreams at once. Simple methods:

Spacing Out Commitments: Ensuring enough free evenings or weekends to rest or enjoy playful downtime.

Physical Activity They Love: From dance workouts to mild outdoor adventures, movement supports mental clarity.

Healthy Sleep Patterns: Even if they want to read or plan late at night, consistent rest is key to sustained productivity.

Short Digital Detoxes: Taking breaks from phones or social platforms prevents information overload, letting them refocus on real-life tasks.

Caring for mind and body ensures they reach their goals without burning out along the way.

Flexible Timelines for Goals

Sagittarius is not typically fond of strict deadlines. They do better with flexible timelines that still have enough structure to keep them moving:

Progressive Stages: "In six months, I'd like to complete half of my tasks; in a year, I'd like to see X results."

Checkpoints Instead of Fixed Dates: For creative or personal goals, they might say, "I'll move to the next phase when I'm satisfied with the current one," while still keeping a rough outer limit.

Public Milestones for Accountability: Sharing a rough date with friends can give them a gentle push to meet it.

Room for Course Corrections: If they discover a better method, adjusting the timeline to incorporate new insights can be beneficial.

This approach respects their love for spontaneity while preventing indefinite stalling.

Celebrating Achievements and Looking Ahead

When Sagittarians reach a milestone—like finishing a training program, hitting a savings target, or completing a creative work—they can:

Mark the Achievement: Maybe a personal treat, a gathering with close ones, or a short reflective post describing the journey so far.

Record the Lessons Learned: Writing down what worked can guide future endeavors.

Plan the Next Step (Gently): After one success, they might pick a fresh angle to explore, ensuring continuous growth.

Recognizing each milestone keeps them from rushing so fast that they forget to appreciate their efforts. It also replenishes motivation for upcoming adventures.

Accepting the Unknown

The future is never entirely certain. Sagittarians can embrace this reality with an open mind:

Build Adaptive Skills: Problem-solving, communication, and emotional resilience serve them in any environment.

Maintain a Core Vision: While details may shift, a guiding principle—like "I want to keep learning, help others, and stay open to new experiences"—remains steady.

Be Ready to Pivot: If a plan unravels, they can still trust their ability to regroup, forging a new route toward similar goals.

Practice Gratitude for the Present: Focusing too heavily on the future might overshadow current joys. Taking moments to appreciate what they have right now balances forward focus with present contentment.

This acceptance prevents fear of the unknown from stalling their progress, turning unpredictability into an adventure rather than a threat.

Conclusion

Sagittarians look forward with a sense of possibility. They imagine varied paths and are not afraid of switching direction if they spot something more aligned with their spirit. The future, for them, is a space where they can refine skills, deepen wisdom, meet new cultures, build warm relationships, and create projects that reflect their best qualities. Yet optimism alone does not guarantee success. As we have seen, merging hope with practical steps—whether in finances, career, or family life—ensures that big dreams do not fizzle out when faced with daily realities.

Through flexible planning, clear goals, and consistent effort, a Sagittarius can navigate each stage of life—adolescence, midlife transitions, or retirement—remaining bright, resourceful, and open-hearted. They can adapt to changing conditions, find fresh interests, and keep spreading encouragement to those around them. Confident in their ability to learn and regroup, they approach tomorrow as a wide field of options rather than a source of dread. By caring for personal well-being, nurturing important connections, and managing tasks thoughtfully, the Archer's future brims with meaningful possibilities.

Help Us Share Your Thoughts!

Dear reader,

Thank you for spending your time with this book. We hope it brought you enjoyment and a few new ideas to think about. If there was anything that didn't work for you, or if you have suggestions on how we can improve, please let us know at **kontakt@skriuwer.com**. Your feedback means a lot to us and helps us make our books even better.

If you enjoyed this book, we would be very grateful if you left a review on the site where you purchased it. Your review not only helps other readers find our books, but also encourages us to keep creating more stories and materials that you'll love.

By choosing Skriuwer, you're also supporting **Frisian**—a minority language mainly spoken in the northern Netherlands. Although **Frisian** has a rich history, the number of speakers is shrinking, and it's at risk of dying out. Your purchase helps fund resources to preserve and promote this language, such as educational programs and learning tools. If you'd like to learn more about Frisian or even start learning it yourself, please visit **www.learnfrisian.com**.

Thank you for being part of our community. We look forward to sharing more books with you in the future.

Warm regards,
The Skriuwer Team